SpringerBriefs in Intelligent Systems

Artificial Intelligence, Multiagent Systems, and Cognitive Robotics

This series covers the entire research and application spectrum of intelligent systems, including artificial intelligence, multiagent systems, and cognitive robotics. Typical texts for publication in the series include, but are not limited to, state-of-the-art reviews, tutorials, summaries, introductions, surveys, and in-depth case and application studies of established or emerging fields and topics in the realm of computational intelligent systems. Essays exploring philosophical and societal issues raised by intelligent systems are also very welcome.

Martin Lackner · Piotr Skowron

Multi-Winner Voting
with Approval Preferences

 Springer

Martin Lackner [iD]
Institute of Logic and Computation
TU Wien
Vienna, Austria

Piotr Skowron [iD]
Faculty of Mathematics, Informatics
and Mechanics
University of Warsaw
Warsaw, Poland

ISSN 2196-548X   ISSN 2196-5498 (electronic)
SpringerBriefs in Intelligent Systems
ISBN 978-3-031-09015-8   ISBN 978-3-031-09016-5 (eBook)
https://doi.org/10.1007/978-3-031-09016-5

This Springer imprint is published by the registered company Springer Nature Switzerland AG
The registered company address is: Gewerbestrasse 11, 6330 Cham, Switzerland

Preface

Multi-Winner voting is the process of selecting a fixed-size set of representative candidates based on voters' preferences. It occurs in applications ranging from politics (parliamentary elections) to the design of modern computer applications (collaborative filtering, dynamic Q&A platforms, diversifying search results). All these applications share the problem of identifying a representative subset of alternatives—and the study of Multi-Winner voting is the principled analysis of this task.

This book provides a thorough and in-depth look at Multi-Winner voting based on approval preferences. One speaks of approval preferences if voters express their preferences by providing a set of candidates they approve. Approval preferences thus separate candidates in approved and disapproved ones, a simple, binary classification. The corresponding Multi-Winner voting rules are called Approval-Based Committee (ABC) rules. Due to the simplicity of approval preferences, ABC rules are widely suitable for practical use.

Recent years have seen a rising interest in ABC voting. While Multi-Winner voting has been originally a topic studied by economists and political scientists, a significant share of the recent progress has occurred in the field of *computational social choice*. This discipline is situated at the intersection of artificial intelligence, computer science, economics, and (to a lesser degree) political science, combining insights and methods from these distinct fields. The goal of this book is to present fundamental concepts and results for ABC voting and to discuss the recent advances in computational social choice. The main focus is on axiomatic analysis, algorithmic results, and relevant applications.

Vienna, Austria   Martin Lackner
Warsaw, Poland   Piotr Skowron

Acknowledgments

First and foremost, we would like to thank Piotr Faliszewski for extensive feedback and discussions that significantly improved this book. We are further very thankful to Markus Brill, Svante Janson, Jérôme Lang, Marie-Louise Lackner, Jean-François Laslier, Jan Maly, Dominik Peters, and Luis Sánchez-Fernández for providing valuable feedback and comments.

Martin Lackner was supported by the Austrian Science Fund (FWF): P31890. Piotr Skowron was supported by Poland's National Science Center grant UMO-2019/35/B/ST6/02215.

Contents

Chapter 1
Approval-Based Committee Voting

1.1 Introduction

What is multi-winner voting? In a multi-winner election, we are given a set of candidates, a set of voters, the preferences that each voter has over these candidates, and a desired size k of the committee to be elected. The goal is to select a committee of exactly k candidates based on the voters' preferences.

Using this broad understanding of what multi-winner elections are, we encounter them in many vastly different scenarios ranging from everyday life to technical applications. A prototypical multi-winner election is the democratic selection of a representative body, such as a parliament,[1] a faculty council, or a board of trustees. Moreover, selecting finalists in a competition, based on judgements of experts, is also an instance of multi-winner elections—here the experts act as voters and the contestants as candidates. Other possible applications of multi-winner election rules have been identified in the artificial intelligence, economics, and broader computer science literature:

1. finding group recommendations [29, 30, 32], where the possible recommendations can be thought of as candidates and individual group members as voters,
2. collaborative filtering [11, 18], where, for example, related movies are recommended based on large data collections,

---

[1] Most countries use legislatures based on political parties for electing parliaments. However, in some countries open-list systems are used (e.g., in Austria, Belgium, Finland, Latvia, Luxembourg, Netherlands, Sweden, and Switzerland); these systems (also) allow voters to vote for individual candidates rather than only for political parties. Indeed, a few important arguments for allowing to vote for individual candidates have been raised. For example, when voting for individual candidates, the elected candidates are more committed to the electorate rather than to their political parties. At the same time, open-list systems allow the candidates to focus on campaigning for the citizens' votes rather than on gaining influence within their party [2, 3, 12, 13]. For a more general, comparative analysis of different electoral systems, we refer the reader to the relevant political science literature [17, 20, 28, 31].

© The Author(s) 2023
M. Lackner and P. Skowron, *Multi-Winner Voting with Approval Preferences*,
SpringerBriefs in Intelligent Systems, https://doi.org/10.1007/978-3-031-09016-5_1

Fig. 1.1 An approval ballot. Here, the voter decided to approve two of the five candidates. In this hypothetical election, the five candidates are 19th-century academics who are relevant to this book

Victor D'Hondt	☒
Gustaf Eneström	☐
Vilfredo Pareto	☐
L. Edvard Phragmén	☒
Thorvald N. Thiele	☐

3. diversifying search results [33], where users sending a search query can be interpreted as voters and the possible search results correspond to candidates,
4. locating public facilities [16, 32], where the candidates are possible locations in which facilities can be built,
5. the design of dynamic Q&A platforms [21], where participants propose and upvote questions to be asked in a Q&A session,
6. selecting validators in consensus protocols (blockchain) [9, 10], with the users of the protocol corresponding to both voters and candidates, and
7. genetic programming [14], a technique to solve global optimisation problems.

The outcome of a multi-winner election should clearly depend on the available preference information. In a political election, this preference information is typically elicited with (paper) ballots; in a computer application, this information is shaped by the design of the user interface. In this book, we are looking at the approval-based model of multi-winner elections. The approval-based model is based on the assumption that the available preference information for each voter is a separation between approved and non-approved candidates, as illustrated in Fig. 1.1. That is, each voter submits *approval preferences* via a subset of candidates—this subset consists of the candidates approved by the voter.[2] The main object of this book are approval-based committee voting rules (ABC voting rules), i.e., functions that select one or more committees given an approval-based multi-winner election. Importantly, we require that ABC voting rules are deterministic (and not randomised).

To illustrate a multi-winner election with approval preferences, consider the following simple example. There are 100 voters and 5 candidates a,b,c,d,e: 66 voters approve the set $\{a, b, c\}$, 33 voters approve $\{d\}$, and one voter approves $\{e\}$. Assume we want to select a committee of size three. If we count by how many voters each candidate is approved, we see that a, b, and c are approved most often (66 times). This can be seen as a good reason to choose the committee $\{a, b, c\}$ based on these preferences; this committee contains the "strongest" candidates. Note, however, that this committee essentially ignores the preferences of 34 voters. Instead, one could choose the committee $\{a, d, e\}$, in which every voter finds one approved candidate.

---

[2] The other main variant of multi-winner elections is based on rankings, where each voter orders the candidates from the most to the least preferred one. We only briefly consider ranking-based multi-winner elections in this book (Sect. 6.1)—for a more substantial overview we refer the reader to a book chapter by Faliszewski et al. [15].

A more proportional committee would be $\{a, b, d\}$: here, the 66 voters approving $\{a, b, c\}$ (which are roughly two-thirds of the population) have two approved candidates in the committee (two-thirds of the committee). All of these committees are sensible and it is easy to find arguments for and against them. For now, let us just observe that we need a principled way in which we can distinguish the properties of committees and ABC voting rules.

In recent years, much progress has been made in the field of ABC elections. This can be seen when comparing the content of this book with the comprehensive overviews by Kilgour [22] and Kilgour and Marshall [23], published in 2010 and 2012, respectively. Indeed, multi-winner elections have been extensively studied from the perspective of economics (in the field of *social choice theory* [22, 23]), political science (in the context of political elections and voting systems [17, 31]) and artificial intelligence (in the field of *computational social choice* [8]). The goal of this book is to provide an up-to-date summary of the state of the art. A particular focus is put on axiomatic and algorithmic analysis; this line of work is prevalent in social choice theory and computational social choice.

Broadly speaking, we want to answer two main questions in this book:

(1) What are the main properties of established ABC rules? Based on which principles can one choose a good ABC rule for a given application? (The answer to this question usually depends on the types of properties that the reader considers particularly important for his or her application.)
(2) What are the practical limitations of using a particular rule, and how can one deal with these limitations? This question encompasses, e.g., algorithmic questions regarding computational complexity, and the possibility of conflicting axiomatic properties.

Before we delve into ABC voting rules, let us first take a step back and discuss advantages and disadvantages of making collective decisions based on approval preferences.

1.2 Advantages and Drawbacks of Approval Ballots

There are several arguments for using approval ballots in multi-winner elections (i.e., to work with approval preferences). Compared to the ranking-based model, where voters provide complete rankings of candidates (i.e., linear orders), providing approval preferences requires much less cognitive effort from the voters. Thus this kind of voting is often more practical and preferable due to its clear meaning. Brams and Herschbach [7] and Aragones et al. [4] discuss positive effects of using approval ballots on voters' participation, and Brams and Herschbach [7] further argue that using approval ballots can reduce negative campaigning; Brams and Fishburn [5] discuss other possible positive implications of using approval ballots in political elections. In fact, approval ballots are often used for voting in scientific societies (see, e.g., the work of Brams and Fishburn [6]). Further experimental studies explore the possibility of using approval ballots in political elections and their conclusions are largely positive [1, 26, 27, 34]. Approval ballots are widely used in participatory budgeting [19]. These are elections where the citizens decide through voting how to spend a municipal budget (we discuss this setting in Sect. 6.4).

In general, the approval-based model has the advantage of a simple yet expressive preference model. This simplicity grants definitions of more complex concepts within this model (e.g., proportionality, strategyproofness, etc.) a solid intuitive grounding.

The simplicity of approval ballots necessarily also has downsides. An important underlying assumption is that the preferences of voters are separable, i.e., voters are not given the possibility to specify relations between candidates. For example, it is not possible for a voter to indicate that she believes that a certain group of candidates would work particularly well together in the elected committee or that she thinks that two candidates should never be elected together. We discuss several related models that allow voters to specify this kind of information in Sect. 6.6.

Approval ballots imply a dichotomy between candidates: approved and disapproved candidates. While it is generally clear how to interpret the set of approved candidates, it is less clear how to interpret the set of disapproved candidates, i.e., its complement. Generally, it can be assumed that a voter prefers approved candidates to be included in the winning committee, that is, adding an approved candidate to the committee will increase a voter's satisfaction. For disapproved candidates, the situation is less clear as the voter may be either neutral about whether these candidates are included or opposed to their inclusion (or a mixture of these two cases). As the ABC model does not allow to distinguish between neutral and negative candidates, this information cannot be taken into account by ABC rules. We discuss the trichotomous (three-valued) model in Sect. 6.2. Generally, moving from dichotomous preferences (the ABC model) to trichotomous preferences results in a vastly different model, with its own advantages and disadvantages.

A much more elaborate discussion of the approval-based model can be found in the Handbook of Approval Voting [25].

1.3 Python Code

This book is closely connected with the **abcvoting** Python library [24]. The ABC rules discussed in this book are available as Python code at https://github.com/martinlackner/abcvoting and are directly usable, e.g., in numerical experiments. To give a flavour how **abcvoting** looks like, we show here the code to compute winning committees for Proportional Approval Voting (PAV), an important ABC rule.

```
from abcvoting.preferences import Profile
from abcvoting import abcrules

# a preference profile with 5 candidates (0, 1, 2, 3, 4)
profile = Profile(5)
```

```
# add six voters, specified by the candidates that they approve;
# the first voter approves candidates 0, 1, and 2,
# the second voter approves candidates 0 and 1, etc.
profile.add_voters([{0,1,2}, {0,1}, {0,1}, {1,2}, {3,4}, {3,4}])

# compute winning committees
committees = abcrules.compute_pav(profile, committeesize=3)
```

Many examples from this book are also available in the abcvoting library, including the counterexamples from Appendix A. If the reader prefers a Python-based hands-on approach, this library can be a useful tool.

1.4 Mathematical Notation and Prerequisites

We use the following basic notation. We write $\mathbb{N}$ to denote the set of non-negative integers and $\mathbb{R}$ to denote the set of real numbers. Given a real number x, the *floor function* $\lfloor x \rfloor$ returns the largest integer $\leq x$. Similarly, the *ceiling function* $\lceil x \rceil$ returns the smallest integer $\geq x$. For each $t \in \mathbb{N}$, we let $[t]$ denote the set $\{1, \dots, t\}$. For a set X, we write $|X|$ to denote its cardinality. We further write $\mathcal{P}(X)$ to denote the *powerset* of X, i.e., the set of all subsets of X.

A *weak order* is a binary relation on a set X which is complete and transitive. A *linear order* is a weak order that is antisymmetric; we refer to linear orders also as *rankings*. Observe that weak orders may contain ties between elements (in contrast to linear orders).

We use the standard *asymptotic notation* $O(.)$, $o(.)$ and $\Theta(.)$, denoting upper, lower, and tight bounds up to constant factors, respectively.

We assume that the reader is familiar with basic concepts regarding algorithms (such as polynomial-time vs exponential-time algorithms, the concepts of fixed-parameter and approximation algorithms) and computational complexity theory (such as NP-hardness, NP-completeness, reductions). These concepts are, however, only required for Chap. 5.

1.5 Structure of the Book

This book is structured as follows. In Chap. 2, we give detailed descriptions and examples for many approval-based committee rules. Only parts of this chapter are required for understanding the remainder of the book; these parts are marked with a bar on the side of the page. Chap. 3 provides an overview of basic axiomatic properties of ABC rules. We discuss which of these properties are satisfied by the rules introduced in the previous chapter. In Chap. 4, we focus on a major topic in recent years: proportional representation. We discuss concepts of proportionality (but also concepts of non-proportionality) and their relation to other axiomatic properties. Chap. 5 discusses the computational results concerning the complexity of computing winning committees, and algorithmic questions related to proportionality and strategyproofness. In Chap. 6, we provide an overview of related formalisms and their connection to ABC rules. Finally, in Chap. 7, we provide an outlook on important research directions and list some specific open questions. This book contains a technical appendix, Appendix A, with proofs and counterexamples that we were not able to find in the published literature.

References

1. C. Alós-Ferrer and Đ.-G. Granić. Two field experiments on Approval Voting in Germany. *Social Choice and Welfare*, 39(1):171–205, 2012.
2. B. Ames. Electoral strategies under open-list proportional representation. *American Journal of Political Science*, 39(2):406–433, 1995.
3. A. André, S. Depauw, and S. Martin. Electoral systems and legislators' constituency effort: The mediating effect of electoral vulnerability. *Comparative Political Studies*, 48(4):464–496, 2015.
4. E. Aragones, I. Gilboa, and A. Weiss. Making statements and approval voting. *Theory and decision*, 71(4):461–472, 2011.
5. S. J. Brams and P. C. Fishburn. *Approval Voting*. Birkhäuser, 1983.
6. S. J. Brams and P. C. Fishburn. Going from theory to practice: The mixed success of approval voting. In J.-F. Laslier and M. R. Sanver, editors, *Handbook on Approval Voting*, pages 19–37. Springer, 2010.
7. S. J. Brams and D. R. Herschbach. The science of elections. *Science*, 292(5521):1449, 2001.
8. F. Brandt, V. Conitzer, U. Endriss, J. Lang, and A. D. Procaccia. *Handbook of Computational Social Choice*. Cambridge University Press, New York, NY, USA, 1st edition, 2016.
9. J. Burdges, A. Cevallos, P. Czaban, R. Habermeier, S. Hosseini, F. Lama, H. K. Alper, X. Luo, F. Shirazi, A. Stewart, and G. Wood. Overview of Polkadot and its design considerations. *CoRR*, abs/2005.13456, 2020. URL https://arxiv.org/abs/2005.13456.
10. A. Cevallos and A. Stewart. A verifiably secure and proportional committee election rule. In *Proceedings of the 3rd ACM Conference on Advances in Financial Technologies*, pages 29–42, 2021.
11. A. Chakraborty, G. K. Patro, N. Ganguly, K. P. Gummadi, and P. Loiseau. Equality of voice: Towards fair representation in crowdsourced top-k recommendations. In *Proceedings of the Conference on Fairness, Accountability, and Transparency, FAT* 2019*, pages 129–138. ACM, 2019. 10.1145/3287560.3287570. URL https://doi.org/10.1145/3287560.3287570.
12. E. Chang. Electoral incentives for political corruption under open-list proportional representation. *The Journal of Politics*, 67(3):716–730, 2005.
13. J. M. Colomer. *Personal Representation: The Neglected Dimension of Electoral Systems*. ECPR Press, Colchester, 2011.
14. P. Faliszewski, J. Sawicki, R. Schaefer, and M. Smolka. Multiwinner voting in genetic algorithms. *IEEE Intell. Syst.*, 32(1):40–48, 2017.
15. P. Faliszewski, P. Skowron, A. Slinko, and N. Talmon. Multiwinner voting: A new challenge for social choice theory. In U. Endriss, editor, *Trends in Computational Social Choice*, chapter 2, pages 27–47. AI Access, 2017.
16. F. Z. Farahani and M. Hekmatfar, editors. *Facility Location: Concepts, Models, and Case Studies*. Springer, 2009.
17. D. Farrell. *Electoral systems: A comparative introduction*. Palgrave Macmillan, 2011.
18. G. Gawron and P. Faliszewski. Using multiwinner voting to search for movies. In *Proceedings of the 3rd Games, Agents, and Incentives Workshop (GAIW 2021)*. IFAAMAS, 2021.

19. A. Goel, A. K. Krishnaswamy, S. Sakshuwong, and T. Aitamurto. Knapsack voting. *Collective Intelligence*, 1, 2015.
20. B. Grofman. Perspectives on the comparative study of electoral systems. *Annual Review of Political Science*, 19:1–23, 2016.
21. J. Israel and M. Brill. Dynamic proportional rankings. In *Proceedings of the 30th International Joint Conference on Artificial Intelligence (IJCAI-2021)*, pages 261–267, 2021.
22. D. M. Kilgour. Approval balloting for multi-winner elections. In J.-F. Laslier and M. R. Sanver, editors, *Handbook on Approval Voting*, pages 105–124. Springer, 2010.
23. D. M. Kilgour and E. Marshall. Approval balloting for fixed-size committees. In D. S. Felsenthal and M. Machover, editors, *Electoral Systems: Paradoxes, Assumptions, and Procedures*, Studies in Choice and Welfare, chapter 12, pages 305–326. Springer, 2012.
24. M. Lackner, P. Regner, B. Krenn, and S. S. Forster. abcvoting: A Python library of approval-based committee voting rules, 2021. URL https://doi.org/10.5281/zenodo.3904466. Current version: https://github.com/martinlackner/abcvoting.
25. J.-F. Laslier and M. R. Sanver, editors. *Handbook on Approval Voting*. Springer, 2010.
26. J.-F. Laslier and K. Van der Straeten. A live experiment on approval voting. *Experimental Economics*, 11(1):97–105, 2008.
27. J.-F. Laslier and K. Van der Straeten. Strategic voting in multi-winners elections with approval balloting: a theory for large electorates. *Social Choice and Welfare*, 47(3):559–587, 2016.
28. A. Lijphart and B. Grofman. *Choosing an Electoral System: Issues and Alternatives*. Praeger, New York, 1984.
29. T. Lu and C. Boutilier. Budgeted social choice: From consensus to personalized decision making. In *Proceedings of the 22nd International Joint Conference on Artificial Intelligence (IJCAI-2011)*, pages 280–286, 2011.
30. T. Lu and C. Boutilier. Value directed compression of large-scale assignment problems. In *Proceedings of the 29th Conference on Artificial Intelligence (AAAI-2015)*, pages 1182–1190, 2015.
31. A. Renwick and J. B. Pilet. *Faces on the Ballot: The Personalization of Electoral Systems in Europe*. Oxford University Press, 2016.
32. P. Skowron, P. Faliszewski, and J. Lang. Finding a collective set of items: From proportional multirepresentation to group recommendation. *Artificial Intelligence*, 241:191–216, 2016.
33. P. Skowron, M. Lackner, M. Brill, D. Peters, and E. Elkind. Proportional rankings. In *Proceedings of the 26th International Joint Conference on Artificial Intelligence (IJCAI-2017)*, pages 409–415, 2017.
34. K. Van der Straeten, R. Lachat, and J.-F. Laslier. Strategic voting in multi-winner elections with approval balloting: An application to the 2011 regional government election in Zurich. In J. Aldrich, A. Blais, and L. Stephenson, editors, *The Many Faces of Strategic Voting*. CBS, 2018.

Chapter 2
Dramatis Personae: ABC Rules

In this chapter, we define the basic ingredients of approval-based committee (ABC) voting: candidates, voters, preferences, and committees. Most importantly, we present the main characters of this book: ABC voting rules. We introduce and define the most important ABC rules and discuss the main classes they belong to. These include Thiele methods and their sequential variants, Monroe's rule, Phragmén's rules and its derivatives, as well as non-standard ABC rules.

2.1 The Formal Model

We now define the basic ingredients of approval-based committee (ABC) voting: candidates, voters, preferences, committees, and ABC rules.

2.1.1 Candidates, Voters, and Preferences

Let C be a finite set of available *candidates* (also called *alternatives*). We assume that voters' preferences are available in the form of *approval preferences*, i.e., voters distinguish between alternatives they approve and those that they disapprove—due to this dichotomy such preferences are also called *dichotomous preferences*. Hence a voter's preference over candidates can be represented by a set of approved alternatives. Let $N \subseteq \mathbb{N}$ denote a finite set of *voters*.

An *approval profile* is the collection of all voters' preferences; formally it is a function $A : N \to \mathcal{P}(C)$. We say that $A(i) \subseteq C$ is *voter i's approval ballot*. Throughout the book, we use $n = |N|$ to denote the number of voters and $m = |C|$ to denote the number of alternatives. Further, we write $N(c)$ to denote the subset of voters that approve candidate c, i.e., $N(c) = \{i \in N : c \in A(i)\}$.

© The Author(s) 2023
M. Lackner and P. Skowron, *Multi-Winner Voting with Approval Preferences*,
SpringerBriefs in Intelligent Systems, https://doi.org/10.1007/978-3-031-09016-5_2

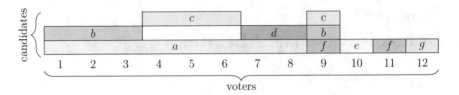

Fig. 2.1 Graphical representation of the approval profile from Example 2.1. Each candidate is represented by one or several boxes that appear in a single row in the figure, and that are marked with a candidate-specific colour. A voter approves those candidates whose corresponding boxes appear above the voter. For example, voter 1 approves candidates a and b and voter 4 approves candidates a and c

Example 2.1 An academic society chooses a steering committee. Such a committee consists of four persons ($k = 4$) and there are seven candidates competing for these positions, $C = \{a, b, c, d, e, f, g\}$. All members of the society are eligible to vote and may provide approval ballots to indicate their preference. In total, 12 ballots have been submitted ($N = [12]$):

$$A(1): \{a, b\} \qquad A(2): \{a, b\} \qquad A(3): \{a, b\} \qquad A(4): \{a, c\}$$
$$A(5): \{a, c\} \qquad A(6): \{a, c\} \qquad A(7): \{a, d\} \qquad A(8): \{a, d\}$$
$$A(9): \{b, c, f\} \qquad A(10): \{e\} \qquad A(11): \{f\} \qquad A(12): \{g\}.$$

Figure 2.1 shows a graphical representation of this approval profile. In this figure, each column correspond to one voter (one approval set) and each candidate appears in only one row—each candidate is approved by the voters that appear below the boxes that represent the candidate. Colours are used to distinguish different candidates.

Sometimes, we are only interested in how often a specific approval set occurs in an approval profile and thus ignore the names (identifiers) of the voters who cast the approval ballots. In such cases, we do not specify the concrete mapping from N to approval sets but use the following notation:

$$3 \times \{a, b\} \qquad 3 \times \{a, c\} \qquad 2 \times \{a, d\} \qquad 1 \times \{b, c, f\}$$
$$1 \times \{e\} \qquad 1 \times \{f\} \qquad 1 \times \{g\}.$$

The reader may ponder which steering committee of size $k = 4$ should be selected given this approval profile—there is certainly more than one sensible choice. In the following chapter, we will see how different voting rules decide in this situation.

We do not make assumptions about the size of approval ballots, as we assume that it is the voters' decision how many candidates she approves. In applications, however, there is sometimes an upper limit on how many candidates can be approved (often the desired committee size). Such a requirement has hardly any effect on the results presented in this book. In a richer model where voters have underlying, non-dichotomous (i.e., non-binary) preferences, such a restriction would become more relevant; this effect has been analysed by Xiao et al. [47] and Godziszewski et al. [20]. The main conclusion is that it is typically better to give the voters freedom in choosing how many candidates they wish to approve.

2.1.2 Committees and ABC Rules

As we have seen in Example 2.1, committees are sets of candidates. Typically, we are interested in committees of a specific size, which we denote by k. The input for choosing such a committee is an *election instance* $E = (A, k)$ consisting of a preference profile A and a desired committee size k. Note that given A, we can derive N and C from this function: N is the domain of A and—under the mild assumption that all candidates are approved by at least one voter—C is the union of all function values, i.e., $C = \bigcup_{i \in N} A(i)$. Thus we do not mention N and C in this notation.

Let us now define the key concept of this book: *approval-based committee voting rules* (short: *ABC rules*). An ABC rule is a voting method for choosing committees, i.e., an ABC rule takes an election instance as input and outputs one or more size-k subsets of candidates. We refer to these size-k subsets as *winning committees*.

If an ABC rule outputs more than one committee, we say that these committees are *tied*. An ABC rule is *resolute* if it always outputs exactly one committee. In practical settings, it is often undesirable to have more than one winning committee. Consequently, in many concrete voting systems a tiebreaking method is included so that a resolute outcome is guaranteed. This tiebreaking method is typically a random process. As we assume that an ABC rule is a deterministic process, we further assume that all randomisation is done before the election (or at least before the ABC rule is applied). Under this assumption, a randomised tiebreaking method corresponds to a fixed (linear) tiebreaking order over committees; if more than one committee is winning, this tie is resolved by picking the winning committee that is maximal in the tiebreaking order. In this sense, our model incorporates voting systems that rely on randomised tiebreaking.[1]

Some of the ABC rules defined in the following are resolute, i.e., they always return a single winning committee, and some are irresolute. Most rules can be defined either way; we have chosen the more natural definition for each rule.

For the following definitions, we assume that we are given an election instance $E = (A, k)$ with a voter set N and a candidate set C.

2.2 Thiele Methods

In the single-winner setting, i.e., if $k = 1$, there are few reasonable voting rules when presented with approval ballots. The arguably most natural rule is Approval Voting. Approval Voting selects those alternatives that are approved by the maximum number of voters, all of which are (co-)winners according to this rule. Most ABC rules introduced in this chapter are equivalent to Approval Voting for the case $k = 1$ (we discuss notable exceptions in Sect. 2.7). There is, however, one ABC rule that

---

[1] For a more careful study of randomised tie-breaking, one would have to model the outcome of a randomised ABC rule as a probability distribution over potentially winning committees. Note that this distribution is not necessarily uniform.

extends the reasoning of Approval Voting to $k > 1$ in the most natural manner; this rule is therefore called Multi-Winner Approval Voting (short: AV).[2]

Rule 1 (Multi-Winner Approval Voting, AV) *This ABC rule selects the k candidates which are approved by most voters. Formally, the AV-score of an alternative $c \in C$ is defined as* $\text{score}_{AV}(A, c) = |N(c)| = |\{i \in N : c \in A(i)\}|$ *and AV selects committees W that maximise* $\text{score}_{AV}(A, W) = \sum_{c \in W} \text{score}_{AV}(A, c)$.

Example 2.2 Let us consider the instance of Example 2.1:

$$3 \times \{a, b\} \quad 3 \times \{a, c\} \quad 2 \times \{a, d\} \quad 1 \times \{b, c, f\} \quad 1 \times \{e\} \quad 1 \times \{f\} \quad 1 \times \{g\}.$$

To compute winning committees according to AV, we count how often each alternative is approved: a: 8 times, b: 4, c: 4, d: 2, e: 1, f: 2 and g: 1. We want to select the four most-approved alternatives. These are a, b, c, and there is a tie between d and f (both having the fourth highest number of approvals). Hence, AV returns two tied committees: the sets $W_1 = \{a, b, c, d\}$ and $W_2 = \{a, b, c, f\}$. It is noteworthy that W_1 leaves three voters completely unsatisfied with the chosen alternatives, whereas W_2 results in only two completely unsatisfied voters.

We continue with an ABC rule that can be seen as the exact opposite of AV. Whereas AV disregards whether some voters completely disagree with a committee, the Approval Chamberlin–Courant rule grants as many voters as possible at least one approved alternative in the committee. This rule was first mentioned by Thiele[3] [44], and then independently introduced in a different context by Chamberlin and Courant [12].

Rule 2 (Approval Chamberlin–Courant, CC) *The CC rule outputs all committees W that maximise* $\text{score}_{CC}(A, W) = |\{i \in N : A(i) \cap W \neq \emptyset\}|$.

Example 2.3 Considering again the instance of Example 2.1, there is exactly one committee that grants each voter (at least) one approved candidate: $W = \{a, e, f, g\}$. This is the winning committee according to Approval Chamberlin–Courant. While this committee indeed provides some satisfaction for every voter, it includes alternatives (e and g) that are approved only by single voters.

---

[2] Let us briefly mention variants of AV that are widely used in political settings: Block Voting, where voters may not approve more than k candidates (or sometimes exactly k), Limited Voting, where voters may approve at most s candidates with $s < k$, and Single Non-Transferable Vote (SNTV), which is Limited Voting for $s = 1$. Note that properties of AV do not necessarily transfer to these input-restricted variants and vice-versa. For example, forcing voters to approve exactly k candidates appears to have severe negative consequences, as demonstrated by Elkind et al. [14] in numerical experiments. In this book we consider only AV, which allows arbitrary approval ballots as input.

[3] Thorvald Nicolai Thiele (1838–1910) was a Danish astronomer and mathematician. He was professor of astronomy at the University of Copenhagen and director of the Copenhagen University Observatory. He is most known for his work in mathematics, in particular in statistics [26, 30, 45, 46]. The contributions of Thiele to voting theory are discussed in detail by Janson [22].

The two ABC rules we discussed so far—AV and CC—can be seen as extreme points in the spectrum of ABC rules captured by the class of *Thiele methods*. This class, introduced by Thiele in the late 19th century [44], encompasses all rules that maximise the sum of the voters' individual satisfaction, subject to a chosen definition of how satisfaction is measured. The unifying assumption is that a voters' satisfaction with a committee W is solely determined by the number of approved candidates in this committee, i.e., voter i's satisfaction is determined by a function $w(|W \cap A(i)|)$. By choosing different w-functions, a very broad spectrum of ABC rules can be covered.

Rule 3 (Thiele methods, w-Thiele[4]) *A Thiele method is parameterized by a non-decreasing function $w : \mathbb{N} \to \mathbb{R}$ with $w(0) = 0$. The score of a committee W given a profile A is defined as*

$$\text{score}_w(A, W) = \sum_{i \in N} w(|W \cap A(i)|);$$

the w-Thiele method returns committees with maximum score.

Indeed, AV is the w-Thiele method with $w(x) = x$, and CC is the w-Thiele method with $w(x) = \min(1, x)$. This is an immediate consequence of the respective definitions.

The following Thiele method is arguably one of the most important: Proportional Approval Voting, in short PAV. Also this rule was defined in Thiele's original paper [44]. The definition (and properties) of PAV crucially depend on the sequence of harmonic numbers.

Rule 4 (Proportional Approval Voting, PAV) *Let $h(x) = \sum_{j=1}^{x} 1/j$ denote the sequence of harmonic numbers. PAV is h-Thiele, i.e., it is the w-Thiele rule with $w(x) = h(x)$. In other words, PAV assigns to each committee W the PAV-score, $\text{score}_{PAV}(A, W) = \sum_{i \in N} h(|W \cap A(i)|)$, and returns all committees with maximum score.*

By using the sequence of harmonic numbers $h(\cdot)$, we introduce a flattening satisfaction function for voters, akin to the *law of diminishing returns*. As a consequence, PAV balances the (justified) demands of large groups with the conflicting goal of satisfying small groups. Indeed, as we will see in Chap. 4, Proportional Approval Voting achieves this balance in a proportional fashion. Figure 2.2 shows a visualisation of the defining w-functions of different Thiele methods:

$$w_{AV}(x) = x \qquad w_{PAV}(x) = \sum_{i=1}^{x} 1/i \qquad w_{CC}(x) = \begin{cases} 0 & \text{if } x = 0, \\ 1 & \text{if } x \geq 1. \end{cases}$$

Note that also visually the function defining PAV is "in between" AV and CC.

---

[4] The class of Thiele methods is sometimes also referred to as *weighted PAV rules* [3]; we prefer the term *Thiele methods* as only few rules in this class are actually proportional. Kilgour and Marshall [23] refer to this class as *generalised approval procedures*.

Fig. 2.2 Defining
w-functions for three Thiele
methods: Multi-Winner
Approval Voting (AV),
Proportional Approval
Voting (PAV), and Approval
Chamberlin–Courant (CC)

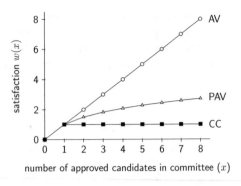

Example 2.4 Given the instance of Example 2.1:

$$3 \times \{a, b\} \quad 3 \times \{a, c\} \quad 2 \times \{a, d\} \quad 1 \times \{b, c, f\} \quad 1 \times \{e\} \quad 1 \times \{f\} \quad 1 \times \{g\},$$

PAV selects the committee $W = \{a, b, c, f\}$. For one voter (the one that approves $\{b, c, f\}$) this committee contains three approved alternatives, for six voters this committee contains two approved alternatives, for three voters W contains one approved alternative, and two voters are not at all satisfied with W. Thus, we have $\text{score}_{\text{PAV}}(A, W) = (1 + 1/2 + 1/3) + 6 \cdot (1 + 1/2) + 3 \cdot 1 = {}^{83}/_6$ and this value is optimal. Coincidentally, W is one of the two committees produced by AV, namely the one with fewer dissatisfied voters. It appears that PAV strives for a compromise between AV and CC—this is an intuition that we will discuss in more detail later (Sect. 4.5).

Other Thiele methods that have been studied in the literature are the class of p-geometric rules [42], threshold procedures [19, 23], and Sainte-Laguë Approval Voting (SLAV) [25].

Thiele methods pick committees that maximise a certain welfare of the voters and thereby belong to a broader class of welfarist rules.

Definition 2.1 A *welfare vector* induced by a committee W specifies, for each voter, her satisfaction from W (measured as the number of candidates she approves in W):

$$\text{welf}(W) = (|A(1) \cap W|, |A(2) \cap W|, \ldots, |A(n) \cap W|).$$

An ABC rule $\mathcal{R}$ is *welfarist* if there is a function $f : \mathbb{N}^N \to \mathbb{R}$, mapping welfare vectors to scores, such that for each instance (A, k) we have

$$\mathcal{R}(A, k) = \underset{W \subseteq C \text{ with } |W| = k}{\arg\max} \ f(\text{welf}(W)).$$

In this definition, $f(\text{welf}(W))$ can be viewed as the welfare that voters gain from W. For Thiele methods, $f(\text{welf}(W)) = \text{score}_w(A, W)$, i.e., welfare is the sum of the voters' w-scores. The class of welfarist rules also allows for an aggregation other than summation. For example, one can define $f(\text{welf}(W))$ as the satisfaction of the least-satisfied voter—akin to egalitarian aggregation [29]. Another example of a welfarist rule is a dictatorial rule which compares welfare vectors lexicographically given a fixed order of voters: the first voter in this order is a dictator and only if the dictator is indifferent between two outcomes, the second-in-place may decide, and so on.

These other forms of aggregation have been studied in the context of multi-winner elections with ranking-based preferences (for the egalitarian aggregation see the work of Aziz et al. [4] and Skowron et al. [41]; for OWA-based aggregation see the work of Elkind and Ismaili [13] and Faliszewski et al. [17]). For approval ballots, we are aware of only two works that consider such aggregations. Computational properties of CC and Monroe rules based on the egalitarian aggregation are considered by Betzler et al. [5]. Amanatidis et al. [1] consider OWA-based aggregation but for other types of welfare of individual voters. Specifically, the satisfaction of voters with a committee is measured via the Hamming distance, which is in contrast to the definition of $\text{welf}(W)$. The most important rule based on the Hamming distance is Minimax Approval Voting, which we discuss in Sect. 2.7.

2.3 Sequential Variants of Thiele Methods

Thiele methods are defined via optimisation statements: given an objective function, Thiele methods return all committees that maximise this function. Instead of computing the true optimum (which is computationally hard, as we will see in Chap. 5), one can define sequential procedures that construct an approximate solution. We define here two classes of sequential procedures: sequential and reverse sequential Thiele methods. Both classes have been introduced in Thiele's original paper [44] (see Janson's survey for further historical remarks [22]). Furthermore, both classes can be seen as greedy approximation algorithms for Thiele methods; we return to this analogy in Sect. 5.2.3.

Let us begin with sequential Thiele methods: starting with an empty committee, they add committee members one by one, in each step the one that increases the objective function the most.

Rule 5 (Sequential w-Thiele, seq-w-Thiele) *For each w-Thiele method, we define its sequential variant, seq-w-Thiele, as follows. We start with an empty committee $W_0 = \emptyset$. In each round $r \in \{1, \ldots, k\}$, we compute $W_r = W_{r-1} \cup \{c\}$, where c is a candidate that maximises $\text{score}_w(A, W_{r-1} \cup \{c\})$, i.e., the candidate that improves the committee's score the most. If more than one candidate yields a maximum score, we break ties according to some given tie-breaking order. The seq-w-Thiele rule returns W_k.*

Two sequential Thiele methods will be of particular interest here: sequential w_{PAV}-Thiele and sequential w_{CC}-Thiele. We refer to these two rules as *seq-PAV* and *seq-CC*. In contrast, the sequential variant of AV (seq-w_{AV}-Thiele) is not relevant to us as it is equivalent to AV. This is because the AV-score (score$_{\mathrm{AV}}$) of candidates is not influenced by the other candidates in the committee.

Example 2.5 Since the instance of Example 2.1 yields the same result for PAV and seq-PAV (and also for CC and seq-CC), we take a look at a different profile:

$$3 \times \{a, b\} \qquad 6 \times \{a, d\} \qquad 4 \times \{b\} \qquad 5 \times \{c\} \qquad 5 \times \{c, d\}.$$

For $k = 2$, PAV selects the committee $\{a, c\}$ with a PAV-score of 19. (Each voter except those that approve only candidate b has exactly one approved candidate in the committee.) Let us contrast this result with seq-PAV. All sequential Thiele methods with $w(1) > 0$, including seq-PAV, select the candidate with the largest number of approvals in the first round—the winner according to (single-winner) Approval Voting. Thus, d is selected in the first round as it gives an AV-score of 11. In the second round, we choose between a (increasing the score by 6) and b (increasing the score by 7) and c (increasing the score by 7.5). Hence, seq-PAV returns the committee $\{c, d\}$ with a PAV-score of 18.5.

Similarly to sequential Thiele methods, *reverse sequential Thiele methods* build committees sequentially, but here one starts with the set of all candidates and sequentially removes the candidate that contributes the least to the committee's score.[5]

Rule 6 (Reverse Sequential w-Thiele, rev-seq-w-Thiele) *For each w-Thiele method, we define its reverse sequential variant, rev-seq-w-Thiele, as follows. We start with $W_m = C$, the set of all candidates. Each round, the candidate with the least marginal contribution to the score is removed. To be precise, in each round r from $m - 1$ down to k, we compute $W_r = W_{r+1} \setminus \{c\}$, where c is a candidate that maximises $\mathrm{score}_w(A, W_{r+1} \setminus \{c\})$, i.e., the candidate whose removal decreases the committee's score the least. If more than one candidate does that, we break ties according to some given tie-breaking order. The rev-seq-w-Thiele rule returns W_k.*

In the remainder of the book, we will only encounter *reverse sequential PAV (rev-seq-PAV)* from the class of Reverse Sequential w-Thiele methods.

Example 2.5 (*continued*) For rev-seq-PAV, we start with the full set of candidates $W_4 = \{a, b, c, d\}$ and remove the candidate with the least marginal contribution: removing a decreases the score by 4.5, removing b decreases the score by 5.5, c by 7.5, and d by 5.5. Thus, a is removed and $W_3 = \{b, c, d\}$. Now, we again compute the marginal contributions: for b it is 7, for c it is 7.5, and for d it is 8.5. We obtain $W_2 = \{c, d\}$, which is the winning committee. We see that for this instance seq-PAV and rev-seq-PAV yield the same winning committee. This does not hold in general.

---

[5] This idea of removing candidates with the lowest score can also be found in ranking-based voting rules such as STV or Baldwin [48].

An election instance where PAV, seq-PAV, and rev-seq-PAV all yield different winning committees can be found in Janson's survey [22, Example 13.3]. The example is due to Thiele [44] and is significantly larger than the examples presented here.

As we have mentioned in Sect. 2.2, most ABC rules coincide with Approval Voting for $k = 1$. Reverse Sequential PAV is an exception. This is, however, not a consequence of the underlying assumptions how ballots are interpreted, but a consequence of how the rule is computed (i.e., in a reverse fashion).

Example 2.6 To see that rev-seq-PAV is a non-standard method, consider the profile:

$$1 \times \{a, b\} \quad 1 \times \{a, b, c\} 1 \times \{a, b, d\} \quad 2 \times \{a, c, d\} \quad 1 \times \{b\} \quad 1 \times \{c\} 1 \times \{d\}.$$

In the first round, the marginal contribution of a is $1/2 + 4 \cdot 1/3$; the marginal contribution from the other candidates is at least 2. Thus, candidate a is removed in the first round, even though it has the highest approval score.

Finally, let us mention a paper by Faliszewski et al. [18] which considers and compares several heuristic algorithms for approximating multi-winner rules (e.g., via simulated annealing). This line of work has not yet been extended specifically to Thiele methods, though the ideas in their work can be applied to the ABC setting.

2.4 Monroe's Rule

Monroe's rule [27] is an ABC rule[6] related to the Chamberlin–Courant rule. It also aims at maximising the number of voters who are represented by at least one candidate in the elected committee. The main difference is that each committee member can represent at most $1/k$-th of the voters.

Rule 7 (Monroe) *Given a committee W, a Monroe assignment for W is a function $\phi: N \to W$ such that each candidate $c \in W$ is assigned roughly the same number of voters, i.e., for all $c \in W$ it holds that $\lfloor n/k \rfloor \le |\phi^{-1}(c)| \le \lceil n/k \rceil$. The candidate $\phi(i)$ can be viewed as the representative of voter i. Let $\Phi(W)$ be the set of all possible Monroe assignments for W. The Monroe-score of a committee W is defined as the number of voters that have a representative assigned that they approve (given an optimal Monroe assignment), i.e., $\text{score}_{\text{Monroe}}(A, W) = \max_{\phi \in \Phi(W)} |\{i \in N : \phi(i) \in A(i)\}|$. Monroe returns all committees with a maximum Monroe score.*

---

[6] Although Monroe defined his rule in the original paper primarily for linear preference orders [27], he considered the modified version based on approval ballots the "most promising option" for actual (political) use. If the distinction between these two rules is necessary, the approval-based version is often denoted as α-Monroe; we do not need this distinction as we focus solely on approval ballots.

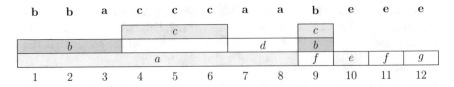

b	b	a	c	c	c	a	a	b	e	e	e

Fig. 2.3 An optimal Monroe assignment for Example 2.7: the top row shows the assigned representative for each voter. For example, the assigned representative of voter 1 is b; voter 12 is dissatisfied with her assigned representative e

Example 2.7 Consider again the profile of Example 2.1:

$A(1)$: $\{a, b\}$ $A(2)$: $\{a, b\}$ $A(3)$: $\{a, b\}$ $A(4)$: $\{a, c\}$

$A(5)$: $\{a, c\}$ $A(6)$: $\{a, c\}$ $A(7)$: $\{a, d\}$ $A(8)$: $\{a, d\}$

$A(9)$: $\{b, c, f\}$ $A(10)$: $\{e\}$ $A(11)$: $\{f\}$ $A(12)$: $\{g\}$.

We first note that the desired committee size $k = 4$ divides the number of voters ($n = 12$) and hence Monroe assigns exactly 3 voters to each committee member. One optimal Monroe assignment (among many) is shown in Fig. 2.3 and given by $\phi^{-1}(a) = \{3, 7, 8\}$, $\phi^{-1}(b) = \{1, 2, 9\}$, $\phi^{-1}(c) = \{4, 5, 6\}$, $\phi^{-1}(e) = \{10, 11, 12\}$. The Monroe score of this assignment is $\text{score}_{\text{Monroe}}(A, W) = 10$, since only voters 11 and 12 are assigned to a representative (candidate e) that they do not approve. In total there are six winning committees; committee $\{a, b, c, e\}$ is one of them.

Monroe's rule has also a natural sequential version called *Greedy Monroe*, which was introduced by Skowron et al. [41].[7] We present Greedy Monroe here in a slightly simpler, more practical fashion, where dissatisfied voters are not assigned to groups.

Rule 8 (Greedy Monroe) *This ABC rule proceeds in k rounds: In each round $r \in \{1, \ldots, k\}$ Greedy Monroe assigns a candidate to a group of voters G_r of size at most n_r (defined below); this candidate is added to the committee. The maximum size of a group, n_r, is defined as follows: for $d = n \mod k$, we set $n_1 = \cdots = n_d = \lceil n/k \rceil$ and $n_{d+1} = \cdots = n_k = \lfloor n/k \rfloor$. In round $r + 1$, let N_{r+1} denote the voters that have not yet an assigned committee member, i.e., $N_{r+1} = N \setminus (G_1 \cup \cdots \cup G_r)$. Candidate c_{r+1} is chosen as the candidate c that maximises $|\{i \in N_{r+1} : c \in A(i)\}|$ among those not contained in the committee yet (using a tiebreaking order on candidates if necessary). Now, if there are at most n_{r+1} not yet assigned voters that approve c_{r+1}, then $G_{r+1} = \{i \in N_{r+1} : c_{r+1} \in A(i)\}$; if there are more than n_{r+1} such voters, a tiebreaking order on voters is used to assign exactly n_{r+1} from these voters to G_{r+1}. Greedy Monroe outputs the committee $\{c_1, \ldots, c_k\}$.*

---

[7] Greedy Monroe is called *Algorithm A* in the original paper [41] and is defined therein only for instances where k divides n. The first general definition was given in [15].

Example 2.8 In our running example (Example 2.1) given by

$$A(1): \{a, b\} \quad A(2): \{a, b\} \quad A(3): \{a, b\} \quad A(4): \{a, c\}$$
$$A(5): \{a, c\} \quad A(6): \{a, c\} \quad A(7): \{a, d\} \quad A(8): \{a, d\}$$
$$A(9): \{b, c, f\} \quad A(10): \{e\} \quad A(11): \{f\} \quad A(12): \{g\},$$

Greedy Monroe first picks candidate a as it is approved by most voters. We assume that ties among voters are broken in increasing order, so $G_1 = \{1, 2, 3\}$. Now c is chosen since it is the only candidate with four supporters among the remaining voters ($N_2 = \{4, \ldots, 12\}$). The corresponding group of voters is $G_2 = \{4, 5, 6\}$ (again choosing voters with smaller indices first). Now there are two candidates left that are approved by two voters in the remaining set ($N_3 = \{7, \ldots, 12\}$): candidates d and f. We choose d by alphabetic tiebreaking and so we set $G_3 = \{7, 8\}$. Finally, there is one candidate that has two supporting voters in $N_4 = \{9, \ldots, 12\}$: f is approved by voters 9 and 11; thus $G_4 = \{9, 11\}$. A Monroe assignment corresponding to this committee $\{a, c, d, f\}$ is, e.g., given by $\phi^{-1}(a) = \{1, 2, 3\}$, $\phi^{-1}(c) = \{4, 5, 6\}$, $\phi^{-1}(d) = \{7, 8, 10\}$, and $\phi^{-1}(f) = \{9, 11, 12\}$. In this instance, Greedy Monroe was able to find a committee with an optimal Monroe score, but this does not hold in general.

2.5 Phragmén's Rules

Phragmén[8] introduced a number of voting rules, most of which are based on a form of cost-sharing (or load balancing). The core idea is that placing a candidate in the winning committee incurs a cost, or load, that has to be shouldered by the voters who approve this candidate. The goal is to choose a committee that allows for as equal as possible a distribution of its cost. In this way, the preferences of as many voters as possible are taken into account.

Phragmén's main proposal is called *Phragmén's Sequential Rule* (seq-Phragmén). Even though Phragmén's Sequential Rule can be considered one of the most appealing ABC rules, it remained unknown to many social choice researchers until recently. Few publications before 2017 mention Phragmén's methods; notable exceptions are a survey by Janson [21] (in Swedish) and a paper by Mora and Oliver [28] (in Catalan). Since 2017 several papers have proven Phragmén's method to be a particularly strong ABC rule, in particular being a proportional ABC rule that is both polynomial-time computable and committee monotone.

---

[8] Lars Edvard Phragmén (1863–1937) [10, 22, 31, 43] was a Swedish mathematician and an actuary. He was a professor of mathematics at Stockholm University and long-time editor of Acta Mathematica. His best known mathematical work is the Phragmén-Lindelöf principle in complex analysis [39], but he also published several works on election methods [34–38] and was involved in Swedish electoral reforms; see Janson's survey [22] for a comprehensive summary of his work on election methods.

We present two (equivalent) formulations of seq-Phragmén. The first is conceptually simpler, while the second gives a clearer picture how the rule is computed in
practice.

Rule 9 (Phragmén's Sequential Rule, seq-Phragmén) *This ABC rule is based on the
assumption that placing a candidate in the winning committee incurs a cost (or a
load) of 1, which is distributed among the set of voters that approve this candidate.*

Continuous formulation: *We assume that each voter has a budget which constitutes
his or her voting power. Voters start with a budget of 0 and this budget continuously
increases as time advances. At time t, the budget of each voter is t. As soon as a group
of voters that jointly approve a candidate has a total budget of 1, the joint candidate
is added to the winning committee. Then the budget of all involved voters is reset
to 0; only voters that do not approve the selected candidate keep their current budget.
This process continues until the committee is filled. If at some point two candidates
could be added to the committee at the same time, a tie-breaking order is used to
decide which candidate is selected.*

Discrete formulation: seq-Phragmén works in rounds; each round one candidate is
added to the committee. Let $y_r(v)$ denote the load assigned to (or cost contributed
by) voter v after round $r \leq k$. We naturally start with $y_0(v) = 0$ for all $v \in N$. Let
$\{c_1, \ldots, c_{r-1}\}$ be the candidates added to the committee in rounds 1 to $r - 1$. To
determine the next candidate c_r to add, we compute for each candidate $c \in C \setminus
\{c_1, \ldots, c_{r-1}\}$ the maximum load that would arise from adding c_r:

$$\ell_r(c) = \frac{1 + \sum_{i \in N(c)} y_{r-1}(i)}{|N(c)|};$$

the load of voters in $N(c)$ would increase to this amount if c were added to the
committee. Note that the load is distributed so that all voters approving c end up
with the same total load; this is so to minimise the maximum load. Now, to keep the
maximum load as small as possible, seq-Phragmén chooses the candidate c with a
minimum $\ell_r(c)$, i.e.,

$$c_r = \underset{c \in C \setminus \{c_1, \ldots, c_{r-1}\}}{\arg\min} \ell_r(c).$$

If two or more candidates yield the same maximum load, a tie-breaking method is
required (typically some fixed order on C). After choosing c_r, the voter loads are
adapted accordingly:

$$y_r(i) = \begin{cases} \ell_r(c_r) & \text{if } i \in N(c_r), \\ y_{r-1}(i) & \text{if } i \notin N(c_r). \end{cases}$$

The rule returns the winning committee $\{c_1, \ldots, c_k\}$.

To see that these two formulations are equivalent, note that for a winning committee $W = \{c_1, \ldots, c_k\}$ (selected in this order) the maximum loads in each round $\ell_r(c_r)$

directly corresponds to the time points at which sufficient budget was available to pay for c_r. From this point of view, the discrete formulation is only the explicit calculation of time points at which sufficient budget is available to place a new candidate in the committee.

Example 2.9 Let us again consider our running example (Example 2.1):

$$3 \times \{a, b\} \qquad 3 \times \{a, c\} 2 \times \{a, d\}$$
$$1 \times \{b, c, f\} \qquad 1 \times \{e\} 1 \times \{f\} \qquad 1 \times \{g\}.$$

We use the continuous formulation to describe the method, but it is easy to repeat the calculations using the discrete formulation. Figure 2.4 shows a visualisation of the procedure, which we will now explain step by step. The first time sufficient budget is available to add a candidate to the committee is at time $t_1 = 1/8$. At this point, voters $\{1, \ldots, 8\}$ can jointly pay for candidate a. Now the budgets of voters 1 to 8 are reset to 0; the remaining voters have a budget of $1/8$ each.

A second candidate can be added to the committee at time $t_2 = 11/32$. Voters 1, 2, 3, 9 approve candidate b; their respective budgets are $(7/32, 7/32, 7/32, 11/32)$ (note that voters 1, 2, and 3 have budgets that are by $1/8$ lower than that of voter 9). At this time, also voters 4, 5, 6, 9 (who all approve candidate c) have a joint budget of 1. We use alphabetic tiebreaking and select b.

Candidate c is then added as a third candidate at time $t_3 = 55/128$. At this point, voters 4, 5, and 6 have budgets of $39/128$, and voter 9 has a budget of $11/128$; that is in total 1. Note that these numbers follow from the fact that voters 4–6 already paid $1/8$ each for selecting candidate a and voter 9 paid $11/32$ for selecting candidate b.

Finally, at time $t_4 = 5/8$ the last candidate, d, is added to the committee. At this point, the two voters approving d (voters 7 and 8) have budgets of $5/8 - 1/8 = 1/2$, in total 1. Thus, seq-Phragmén returns the committee $\{a, b, c, d\}$. When repeating this calculation using the discrete formulation, one obtains the final loads $y_4 = (t_2, t_2, t_2, t_3, t_3, t_3, t_4, t_4, t_3, 0, 0, 0)$.

Phragmén also discussed optimisation-based analogues of seq-Phragmén. These rules are based on choosing a committee that optimises an objective function (in a similar way as Thiele methods optimise an objective function). We will discuss the most notable optimisation-based method: leximax-Phragmén[9] [8, 22, 37].

Rule 10 (Phragmén's Leximax Rule, leximax-Phragmén) *Each candidate in the committee incurs a load (or cost) of 1 which has to be distributed among voters approving this candidate. Given a committee $W = \{c_1, \ldots, c_k\}$, a valid load distribution for W is a function $\ell_W : W \times N \to [0, 1]$ which satisfies (1) if $\ell_W(c, i) > 0$*

---

[9] Phragmén discusses optimisation variants of his rule in [37] and proposes to minimise the maximum load (see [22]); this rule has been referred to as opt-Phragmén or max-Phragmén. Brill et al. [8] show that it is more sensible to use a lexicographic comparison of loads instead of only considering the maximum load. We thus only discuss leximax-Phragmén (referred to as opt-Phragmén in [8]). Further optimisation variants exist, such as minimising the variance of loads [8, 22, 37].

then voter i approves c, and (2) $\sum_{i \in N} \ell_W(c, i) = 1$ for all $c \in W$. Let $\bar{\ell}_W = \left(\sum_{c \in W} \ell_W(c, i) \right)_{i \in N}$ denote the vector of total loads assigned to the voters.

To compare two (valid) load distributions, we use a lexicographic order. Given a valid load distribution ℓ_W for W, let $sort(\bar{\ell}_W)$ denote the tuple $\bar{\ell}_W$ sorted from largest to smallest. Let ℓ_W and $\ell_{W'}$ denote two valid load distributions for committees W and W', respectively. We say that ℓ_W is lexicographically smaller than $\ell_{W'}$ if there exists an index $j \leq |N|$ such that the first j entries of $sort(\bar{\ell}_W)$ and $sort(\bar{\ell}_{W'})$ are equal and the $(j + 1)$-st entry of $sort(\bar{\ell}_W)$ is strictly smaller than the $(j + 1)$-st entry of $sort(\bar{\ell}_{W'})$.

Let $\ell_W^{\min}$ denote a lexicographically smallest valid load distribution for committee W. Then, leximax-Phragmén returns all committees W for which $\ell_W^{\min}$ is lexicographically minimal in the set $\{\ell_{W'}^{\min} : W' \subseteq C \text{ and } |W'| = k\}$. Note that if leximax-Phragmén returns two committees W_1 and W_2, then $sort(\bar{\ell}_{W_1}^{\min}) = sort(\bar{\ell}_{W_2}^{\min})$.

Example 2.10 In our running example, leximax-Phragmén behaves differently than seq-Phragmén. When looking for a committee that has the lexicographically smallest load distribution, we find committee $W = \{a, b, c, f\}$ with $\ell_W^{\min} = (3/8, 3/8, 3/8, 3/8, 3/8, 3/8, 3/8, 3/8, 1/2, 0, 1/2, 0)$. This load distribution is depicted in Figure 2.5. Committee W is the only winning committee; for example, committee $W' = \{a, b, c, d\}$ (the winning committee of seq-Phragmén) has $\ell_{W'}^{\min} = (3/7, 3/7, 3/7, 3/7, 3/7, 3/7, 1/2, 1/2, 3/7, 0, 0, 0)$, which is lexicographically larger.

2.6 Phragmén-Like Rules

We now discuss a very recent addition to the zoo of ABC rules: the Method of Equal Shares [32, 33] (this method had been originally named Rule X). This rule can be viewed as a variant of seq-Phragmén, where the voters are given some budget upfront,

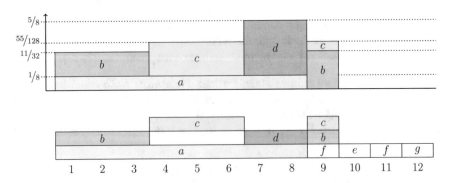

Fig. 2.4 A visualisation of seq-Phragmén (upper part) applied to the election instance of Example 2.1 (lower part). In the upper part all regions of the same colour (corresponding to the same candidate) have an area of 1, which is the budget spent on this candidate

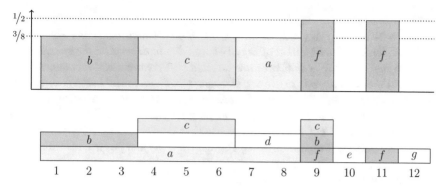

Fig. 2.5 A visualisation of leximax-Phragmén (upper part) applied to the election instance of Example 2.1 (lower part). In the upper part all regions of the same colour (corresponding to the same candidate) have an area of 1, which is the budget spent on this candidate

rather than receiving it continuously. This rule is polynomial-time computable and even surpasses the proportionality guarantees of seq-Phragmén.

Rule 11 (Method of Equal Shares) *The rule proceeds in two phases. The first phase consists of at most k rounds; in each round one candidate is added to the committee. In the second phase the committee is completed in one of several possible ways.*

For the first phase, we assume each voter is initially given a budget of k/n. *Let* $x_r(i)$ *denote the budget of voter i after round r; thus* $x_0(i) = k/n$. *As with seq-Phragmén, putting a candidate in the committee incurs a cost of 1. In round* $r + 1$, *we consider the set of candidates that have not yet been placed in the committee and whose supporters can afford to pay for them, i.e., all candidates c for which* $\sum_{i \in N(c)} x_r(i) \geq 1$. *Let this set be* $C_r \subseteq C$. *If* C_r *is empty, then we conclude the first phase and move to phase two. Otherwise, for each candidate* $c \in C_r$ *we ask what is the minimal budget* $\rho(c)$ *such that each voter approving c pays at most* $\rho(c)$ *and all voters who approve c pay 1 in total, i.e., what is the minimal value* $\rho(c)$ *that satisfies:*

$$\sum_{i \in N(c)} \min(\rho(c), x_r(i)) = 1.$$

(Such a $\rho(c)$ *always exists, since otherwise c would not be contained in* C_r.) *We select the candidate c that minimises* $\rho(c)$ *(using some fixed tiebreaking if necessary), and reduce the budget of voters who approve c accordingly—for each* $i \in N$ *we set*

$$x_{r+1}(i) = \begin{cases} x_i(r) - \rho(c) & \text{if } c \in A(i) \text{ and } x_i(r) \geq \rho(c), \\ 0 & \text{if } c \in A(i) \text{ and } x_i(r) < \rho(c), \\ x_i(r) & \text{if } c \notin A(i), \end{cases}$$

i.e., voters who approve c either pay $\rho(c)$ *or their remaining budget.*

The second phase is only relevant if fewer than k candidates have been put in the committee W so far. If $|W| < k$, we have to add $k - |W|$ additional candidates to W. Many properties of the Method of Equal Shares do not depend on the specific way in which these $k - |W|$ candidates are selected.[10] A concrete and recommendable way to fill the committee is to use seq-Phragmén but with initial budgets defined in the following fashion: When using the continuous formulation, we set the starting budget of each voter to their budget after the first phase of the Method of Equal Shares; this starting budget increases as usual as time advances. Alternatively, we can use the discrete formulation of seq-Phragmén: if the first phase ends with round r', the starting loads are $y_0(i) = -x_{r'}(i)$. Then seq-Phragmén proceeds as usual until the desired committee size is reached.

The name of the rule corresponds to the two elements of its definition. First, each voter is initially given an equal share of the budget that she can spend for "buying" candidates. when a candidate is selected, its cost is split as equally as possible among the voters who approve the candidate (each voter covers an equal share of the cost of the candidate).

Example 2.11 Consider once again our running example. Each voter is initially given a budget of $1/3$. In the first round candidate a is selected and each of the first 8 voters pays $1/8$ for this. In the second round, $C_2 = \emptyset$ since no candidate has sufficiently endowed supporters. For example, the budget of voters who approve b is in total

$$3 \cdot (1/3 - 1/8) + 1/3 < 1$$

and thus insufficient to pay for b. This ends the first phase of the rule.

In the second phase, the voters start receiving additional budget. Voters 1 to 8 start with a budget of $1/3 - 1/8$; voters 9 to 12 start with a budget of $1/3$. At time $t_2 = 1/96$, voters 1 to 8 have a budget of $1/3 - 1/8 + t_2$ each and voters 9 to 12 have a budget of $1/8 + t_2$ each. Hence the voters who approve b (1, 2, 3, 9) have enough money to pay for b:

$$3 \cdot (1/3 - 1/8 + t_2) + (1/3 + t_2) = 1.$$

The same is true for the voters who approve c. Let us assume that we resolve the tie in favour of b: b is selected and the voters 1, 2, 3 and 9 are left without budget. Next, at time $t_3 = 37/384$ candidate c is selected (voters 4–6 contribute $1/3 - 1/8 + t_3$ and voter 9 contributes $t_3 - t_2$, with the required total of 1). Finally, at time $t_4 = 7/24$ we select d $(2 \cdot (1/3 - 1/8 + t_4) = 1)$. Committee $W = \{a, b, c, d\}$ is the only winning committee. In this example, the Method of Equal Shares returns the same committee as seq-Phragmén.

---

[10] An exception is the priceability axiom, see Sect. 4.3; this axiom is dependent on how to extend the committee to its full size. The proposed completion via seq-Phragmén fulfils priceability.

Since in Example 2.11 only one candidate is selected in the first phase of the Method of Equal Shares, we provide one additional example which better illustrates the first phase of this rule and also shows that seq-Phragmén and the Method of Equal Shares may produce different committees.

Example 2.12 Consider the following approval profile given by

$$A(1) = A(2) = A(3) = \{c, d\} \quad A(4) = A(5) = \{a, b\}$$
$$A(6) = A(7) = \{a, c\} \qquad A(8) = \{b, d\}.$$

The goal is to select a committee of size $k = 3$. Thus, voters start with a budget of $3/8$.

In this example, candidate c is selected in the first round with each approving voter (1, 2, 3, 6, 7) paying $1/5$. Next, candidate a is selected. Voters 4 and 5 contribute $13/40$, voters 6 and 7 contribute their remaining budget ($7/40$). None of the remaining candidates achieves a total budget of 1 and thus the second phase starts. The starting budgets for seq-Phragmén are ($7/40$, $7/40$, $7/40$, $1/20$, $1/20$, 0, 0, $3/8$). At time $t = 1/40$ candidate d is selected: voters 1 to 3 can contribute $7/40 + t = 1/5$ each and voter 8 can contribute the remaining $3/8 + t = 2/5$. Hence, the Method of Equal Shares selects the committee $\{a, c, d\}$. The voters' payments in the two phases are illustrated in Fig. 2.6.

In contrast, seq-Phragmén picks $\{b, c, d\}$. These candidates are selected in order c, b, d at time $t_1 = 1/5$, $t_2 = 1/3$, and $t_3 = 29/60$, respectively.

Let us discuss three further rules that are related to Phragmén's rules. The first is the Expanding Approvals Rule [2]. This rule is defined for weak-order preferences

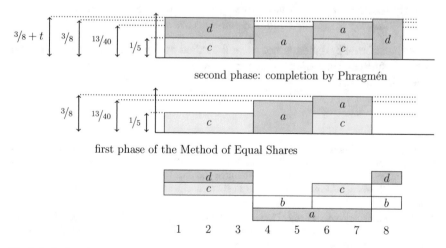

second phase: completion by Phragmén

first phase of the Method of Equal Shares

Fig. 2.6 A visualisation of the Method of Equal Shares applied to the election instance of Example 2.12 (lower part). In the two upper figures, all regions of the same colour (corresponding to the same candidate) have an area of 1, which is the budget spent on this candidate

and has favourable axiomatic properties in this setting. It is less convincing for approval preferences[11] and thus we do not consider it further. The second rule is the maximin support method [40], which is similar to seq-Phragmén. It is an iterative rule based on a form of load balancing, but in contrast to seq-Phragmén all loads can be redistributed each round. A first analysis showed that the maximin support method and seq-Phragmén share many axiomatic properties [40], and a recent manuscript by Cevallos and Stewart [11] shows that the maximin support method provides a constant factor approximation of leximax-Phragmén—in contrast to seq-Phragmén. In the light of the latter paper, one may view the maximin support method as a polynomial-time approximation of leximax-Phragmén (in the same sense as seq-PAV approximates PAV), whereas seq-Phragmén can rather be viewed as a largely independent rule. We focus in this book on seq-Phragmén as it is better studied and conceptually simpler. Still, the maximin support method is an interesting ABC rule that should be analysed in more depth.

Finally, Phragmén also introduced a method now referred to as either Phragmén's first method, Eneström's method, or method of Eneström–Phragmén[12] [9, 16, 22]. This rule can be viewed as an analogue of Single Transferable Vote (STV) with approval ballots.

Rule 12 (Eneström–Phragmén) *This method is based on a quota q, which is typically chosen to be either the Hare quota $q = \frac{n}{k}$ or the Droop quota $q = \frac{n}{k+1}$. Candidates are selected in a sequential fashion. All voters start with a weight of 1. In each round, we compute for each unselected candidate the total weight of approving voters, i.e., the score of an unselected candidate c is the sum of weights of all voters approving c. The candidate with the maximum score is added to the committee (using a tie-breaking if necessary); let this candidate be c' and its score s. Now, the weights are adapted: If $s > q$, then the weights of all voters in $N(c')$ are multiplied by $\frac{s-q}{s}$. Thus, the total weight of voters in $N(c')$ is reduced by q. If $s \leq q$, the weights of voters in $N(c')$ are set to 0. This step is repeated until k candidates are selected.*

As Eneström–Phragmén is not as well studied as Phragmén's rules, we do not discuss it further, but we note that further analysis could prove this rule to be of independent interest.[13]

---

[11] For approval preferences, the Expanding Approvals Rule (EAR) can be rather indecisive. For example, in profiles where no candidate reaches a specified quota and every voter approves only one candidate, EAR selects an arbitrary committee and thus ignores the voters' preferences. For a practical application, EAR would have to be augmented with an additional mechanism that handles such cases.

[12] It is not completely clear whether Phragmén or Gustaf Eneström (1852–1923) should be credited with this method. However, it appears to be justifiable to simply credit both of them; see the historical summary provided by Janson [22, Footnote 38].

[13] The most substantial analysis of Eneström–Phragmén is due to Camps et al. [9]. Most notably, it is not committee monotone (in contrast to seq-Phragmén, cf. Sect. 3.3), but it satisfies proportional justified representation (as seq-Phragmén does, cf. Definition 4.5).

2.7 Non-Standard ABC Rules

As mentioned at the beginning of this chapter, most ABC rules coincide with (single-winner) Approval Voting for $k = 1$. If we understand an approval ballot as indicating those alternatives that a voter likes, then for $k = 1$ it is indeed very natural to select the most-approved alternative. Thus, we refer to rules that differ from Approval Voting for $k = 1$ as *non-standard* ABC rules. In addition to rev-seq-PAV, which we already showed to be non-standard, we present two further non-standard rules. The first one, Minimax Approval Voting (MAV) introduced by Brams et al. [7], interprets approval ballots as the voter's exact description of the desired outcome. If a voter approves a set X, then she indicates that *all* these alternatives should be chosen; any sub- or superset is less desirable. In addition, MAV is an egalitarian rule in the sense that it only pays attention to the least-satisfied voter.

To measure the distance between an approval set and a committee, we rely on the Hamming distance:

Definition 2.2 Given two sets X, Y, we define the Hamming distance between X and Y as the size of their symmetric difference: $d_{ham}(X, Y) = |X \setminus Y| + |Y \setminus X|$.

Rule 13 (Minimax Approval Voting, MAV) *MAV selects committees W that minimise the largest Hamming distance among all voters, i.e., MAV minimises* $\max_{i \in N} d_{ham}(A(i), W)$.

Example 2.13 To see that MAV does not correspond to Approval Voting for $k = 1$, consider the following approval profile:

$$99 \times \{a\} \qquad\qquad 1 \times \{b, c\}.$$

The Hamming distance d_{ham} between the committee $W_1 = \{a\}$ and the approval set $\{b, c\}$ is 3. In contrast, for the committee $W_2 = \{b\}$ (or $\{c\}$) we have $d_{ham}(\{b, c\}, W_2) = 1$ and $d_{ham}(\{a\}, W_2) = 2$. Thus, MAV selects either b or c, even though these alternatives are approved by only a single voter.

Remark 1 It is interesting to note that if we replace the max operator in the definition of MAV by a sum, we obtain the Multi-Winner Approval Voting rule (Rule 1).

Remark 2 MAV, as defined, has a major shortcoming. Consider the following slight modification of Example 2.13:

$$99 \times \{a\} \qquad\qquad 1 \times \{a, b, c\}.$$

For all size-1 committees, the Hamming distance to $\{a, b, c\}$ is 2. Hence, all three committees are equally preferable according to MAV—even though candidate a is approved by every voter (and b and c by only one voter). We see that MAV might disregard a unanimous choice. This problem can be remedied by also considering the second-least satisfied voter in case of ties, and the third-least in case there is still a tie, and so on until a difference between the committees is found. More formally, for each committee W, we compute $d_{\text{ham}}(A(1), W), d_{\text{ham}}(A(2), W), \ldots$ and sort this tuple of length $|N|$ in decreasing order; we denote this tuple of distances D_W. Instead of considering only the first entry in these tuples, we could lexicographically sort them. That is, a committee W_1 is preferred to a W_2 if there exists an index $i \leq n$ such that $D_{W_1}(i) < D_{W_2}(i)$ and $D_{W_1}(j) = D_{W_2}(j)$ for all $1 \leq j < i$. In our example, we have $D_{\{a\}} = (2, 0, 0, \ldots)$ and $D_{\{b\}} = D_{\{c\}} = (2, 2, 2, \ldots)$; with this modification $\{a\}$ is the only winning committee. To the best of our knowledge this modification of MAV has not been studied in the context of voting. However, it is equivalent to the GMAX belief merging operator for the Hamming distance [24].

The second non-standard rule is Satisfaction Approval Voting[14] (SAV). SAV is a variation of AV where each voter has one point and distributes it evenly among all approved candidates. As a consequence, voters who approve more candidates contribute a lesser score to the individual approved candidates.

Rule 14 (Satisfaction Approval Voting, SAV) *The SAV-score of a committee W is defined as*

$$\text{score}_{\text{SAV}}(A, W) = \sum_{i \in N} \frac{|W \cap A(i)|}{|A(i)|}.$$

SAV returns all committees with a maximum SAV-score.

Note that SAV is not a Thiele method since the total number of candidates that a voter approves influences the SAV-score.

Example 2.14 To see that SAV does not correspond to Approval Voting for $k = 1$, consider

$$1 \times \{a\} \qquad\qquad\qquad 3 \times \{b, c, d, e\}.$$

The SAV-score of a is 1 and for b, c, d, and e it is $3/4$. Thus, SAV selects $\{a\}$ even though it is approved by only one voter.

References

1. G. Amanatidis, N. Barrot, J. Lang, E. Markakis, and B. Ries. Multiple referenda and multiwinner elections using Hamming distances: Complexity and manipulability. In *Proceedings of the 14th International Conference on Autonomous Agents and Multiagent Systems (AAMAS-2015)*, pages 715–723, 2015.
2. H. Aziz and B. E. Lee. The expanding approvals rule: Improving proportional representation and monotonicity. *Social Choice and Welfare*, 54(1):1–45, 2020.
3. H. Aziz, M. Brill, V. Conitzer, E. Elkind, R. Freeman, and T. Walsh. Justified representation in approval-based committee voting. *Social Choice and Welfare*, 48(2):461–485, 2017.

---

[14] Satisfaction Approval Voting was introduced under this name by Brams and Kilgour [6], but the method has been discussed already in the 19th century (see Janson's survey [22], Sect. E.1.5.). It is also known as Equal and Even Cumulative Voting.

4. H. Aziz, P. Faliszewski, B. Grofman, A. Slinko, and N. Talmon. Egalitarian committee scoring rules. In *Proceedings of the 27th International Joint Conference on Artificial Intelligence (IJCAI-2018)*, pages 56–62, 2018.
5. N. Betzler, A. Slinko, and J. Uhlmann. On the computation of fully proportional representation. *Journal of Artificial Intelligence Research*, 47:475–519, 2013.
6. S. J. Brams and D. M. Kilgour. Satisfaction approval voting. In *Voting Power and Procedures*, Studies in Choice and Welfare, pages 323–346. Springer, 2014.
7. S. J. Brams, D. M. Kilgour, and M. R. Sanver. A minimax procedure for electing committees. *Public Choice*, 132(3–4):401–420, 2007.
8. M. Brill, R. Freeman, S. Janson, and M. Lackner. Phragmén's voting methods and justified representation. In *Proceedings of the 31st Conference on Artificial Intelligence (AAAI-2017)*, pages 406–413, 2017. Extended version at https://arxiv.org/abs/2102.12305.
9. R. Camps, X. Mora, and L. Saumell. The method of Eneström and Phragmén for parliamentary elections by means of approval voting. *arXiv preprint* arXiv:1907.10590, 2019. URL https://arxiv.org/abs/1907.10590.
10. T. Carleman. L. E. Phragmén in memoriam. *Acta Mathematica*, 69:XXXI–XXXIII, 1938.
11. A. Cevallos and A. Stewart. A verifiably secure and proportional committee election rule. In *Proceedings of the 3rd ACM Conference on Advances in Financial Technologies*, pages 29–42, 2021.
12. B. Chamberlin and P. Courant. Representative deliberations and representative decisions: Proportional representation and the Borda rule. *American Political Science Review*, 77(3):718–733, 1983.
13. E. Elkind and A. Ismaili. OWA-based extensions of the Chamberlin-Courant rule. In *Proceedings of the 4th International Conference on Algorithmic Decision Theory (ADT-2015)*, pages 486–502, 2015.
14. E. Elkind, P. Faliszewski, J. Laslier, P. Skowron, A. Slinko, and N. Talmon. What do multiwinner voting rules do? An experiment over the two-dimensional euclidean domain. In *Proceedings of the 31st Conference on Artificial Intelligence (AAAI-2017)*, pages 494–501, 2017.
15. E. Elkind, P. Faliszewski, P. Skowron, and A. Slinko. Properties of multiwinner voting rules. *Social Choice and Welfare*, 48(3):599–632, 2017.
16. G. H. Eneström. Om aritmetiska och statistiska metoder för proportionella val. *Öfversigt af Kongliga Vetenskaps-Akademiens Förhandlingar*, 53:543–570, 1896.
17. P. Faliszewski, P. Skowron, A. Slinko, and N. Talmon. Multiwinner rules on paths from k-Borda to Chamberlin-Courant. In *Proceedings of the 26th International Joint Conference on Artificial Intelligence (IJCAI-2017)*, pages 192–198. ijcai.org, 2017.
18. P. Faliszewski, M. Lackner, D. Peters, and N. Talmon. Effective heuristics for committee scoring rules. In *Proceedings of the 32nd Conference on Artificial Intelligence (AAAI-2018)*, pages 1023–1030, 2018.
19. P. C. Fishburn and A. Pekeč. Approval voting for committees: Threshold approaches. Technical report, 2004. Technical Report.
20. M. Godziszewski, P. Batko, P. Skowron, and P. Faliszewski. An analysis of approval-based committee rules for 2D-Euclidean elections. In *Proceedings of the 35th Conference on Artificial Intelligence (AAAI-2021)*, pages 5448–5455, 2021.
21. S. Janson. Proportionella valmetoder. Technical report, 2012. Available at http://www2.math.uu.se/~svante/papers/sjV6.pdf.
22. S. Janson. Phragmén's and Thiele's election methods. *CoRR*, abs/1611.08826, 2016. URL http://arxiv.org/abs/1611.08826.
23. D. M. Kilgour and E. Marshall. Approval balloting for fixed-size committees. In D. S. Felsenthal and M. Machover, editors, *Electoral Systems: Paradoxes, Assumptions, and Procedures*, Studies in Choice and Welfare, chapter 12, pages 305–326. Springer, 2012.
24. S. Konieczny and R. P. Pérez. Logic based merging. *Journal of Philosophical Logic*, 40(2):239–270, 2011.
25. M. Lackner and P. Skowron. Utilitarian welfare and representation guarantees of approval-based multiwinner rules. *Artificial Intelligence*, 288:103366, 2020.
26. S. L. Lauritzen. *Thiele: Pioneer in Statistics*. Clarendon Press, 2002.
27. B. Monroe. Fully proportional representation. *American Political Science Review*, 89(4):925–940, 1995.

28. X. Mora and M. Oliver. Eleccions mitjançant el vot d'aprovació. El mètode de Phragmén i algunes variants. *Butlletí de la Societat Catalana de Matemàtiques*, 30(1):57–101, 2015.
29. H. Moulin. *Axioms of Cooperative Decision Making*. Cambridge University Press, 1988.
30. J. J. O'Connor and E. F. Robertson. Thorvald Nicolai Thiele. *MacTutor History of Mathematics*, 2003. URL http://mathshistory.st-andrews.ac.uk/Biographies/Thiele.html.
31. J. J. O'Connor and E. F. Robertson. Lars Edvard Phragmén. *MacTutor History of Mathematics*, 2011. URL http://mathshistory.st-andrews.ac.uk/Biographies/Phragmen.html.
32. D. Peters and P. Skowron. Proportionality and the limits of welfarism. In *Proceedings of the 2020 ACM Conference on Economics and Computation (ACM-EC-2020)*, pages 793–794, 2020. Extended version at https://arxiv.org/abs/1911.11747.
33. D. Peters, G. Pierczynski, and P. Skowron. Proportional participatory budgeting with additive utilities. In *Proceedings of the Thirty-fifth Conference on Neural Information Processing Systems (NeurIPS-2021)*, pages 12726–12737, 2021.
34. E. Phragmén. Om proportionella val. *Stockholms Dagblad*, 14 March 1893, 1893. Summary of a public lecture published in a newspaper.
35. E. Phragmén. Sur une méthode nouvelle pour réaliser, dans les élections, la représentation proportionnelle des partis. *Öfversigt af Kongliga Vetenskaps-Akademiens Förhandlingar*, 51(3):133–137, 1894.
36. E. Phragmén. *Proportionella val. En valteknisk studie*. Svenska spörsmål 25. Lars Hökersbergs förlag, Stockholm, 1895.
37. E. Phragmén. Sur la théorie des élections multiples. *Öfversigt af Kongliga Vetenskaps-Akademiens Förhandlingar*, 53:181–191, 1896.
38. E. Phragmén. Till frågan om en proportionell valmetod. *Statsvetenskaplig Tidskrift*, 2(2):297–305, 1899.
39. E. Phragmén and E. Lindelöf. Sur une extension d'un principe classique de l'analyse et sur quelques propriétés des fonctions monogènes dans le voisinage d'un point singulier. *Acta Mathematica*, 31(1):381–406, 1908.
40. L. Sánchez-Fernández, N. Fernández, J. A. Fisteus, and M. Brill. The maximin support method: An extension of the D'Hondt method to approval-based multiwinner elections. In *Proceedings of the 35th Conference on Artificial Intelligence (AAAI-2021)*, pages 5690–5697, 2021.
41. P. Skowron, P. Faliszewski, and A. Slinko. Achieving fully proportional representation: Approximability result. *Artificial Intelligence*, 222:67–103, 2015.
42. P. Skowron, P. Faliszewski, and J. Lang. Finding a collective set of items: From proportional multirepresentation to group recommendation. *Artificial Intelligence*, 241:191–216, 2016.
43. A. Stubhaug. *Gösta Mittag-Leffler: A man of conviction*. Springer Science & Business Media, 2010.
44. T. N. Thiele. Om flerfoldsvalg. In *Oversigt over det Kongelige Danske Videnskabernes Selskabs Forhandlinger*, pages 415–441. 1895.
45. T. N. Thiele. *Theory of observations*. Charles & Edwin Layton, 1903.
46. T. N. Thiele. *Interpolationsrechnung*. Teubner, Leipzig, 1909.
47. Y. Xiao, H. Deng, X. Lu, and J. Wu. Optimal ballot-length in approval balloting-based multiwinner elections. *Decision Support Systems*, 118:1–9, 2019.
48. W. S. Zwicker. Introduction to the theory of voting. In F. Brandt, V. Conitzer, U. Endriss, J. Lang, and A. D. Procaccia, editors, *Handbook of Computational Social Choice*, pages 23–56. Cambridge University Press, New York, NY, USA, 1st edition, 2016.

Chapter 3
Basic Properties of ABC Rules

In the previous chapter we have seen a wide array of ABC rules. Considering how much they differ in their definitions, it can be expected that they differ also in the properties they exhibit. In this chapter we consider basic properties of ABC rules. These properties describe the behaviour of such rules and offer insights into the nature of specific ABC rules. Table 3.1 offers an overview of most properties discussed in this chapter. This table also includes a rough dichotomy of the rules concerning their computational complexity. Rules that are in P can be computed efficiently, whereas rules that are NP-hard are computationally more demanding; we discuss this dichotomy and further complexity results in Sect. 5.1.

3.1 Anonymity, Neutrality, and Resoluteness

Anonymity and neutrality are two of the most basic properties in the social choice literature [1, 20, 23]. Anonymity states that the identity of voters should not influence the outcome: it should be irrelevant whether voter i approves $A(i)$ and voter j approves $A(j)$ or vice versa. Formally, an ABC rule $\mathcal{R}$ satisfies *anonymity* if for all election instances (A, k) with voter set N and bijections $\pi : N \to N$ it holds that $\mathcal{R}(A, k) = \mathcal{R}(A \circ \pi, k)$. All but one rule introduced in Chap. 2 satisfy anonymity; the exception is Greedy Monroe which uses a fixed tiebreaking order on voters.[1] A typical example of a voting rule that fails anonymity is any dictatorial rule (a rule considering only the preferences of a single distinguished voter, e.g., of voter 1).

Neutrality is the counterpart to anonymity but applies to candidates: it states that all candidates should be treated equally. Formally, an ABC rule $\mathcal{R}$ satisfies *neutrality* if for all election instances (A, k) with candidate set C and bijections $\pi : C \to C$

---

[1] If we defined Greedy Monroe so that it returns all committees that can result from some tiebreaking, then the rule would be anonymous.

© The Author(s) 2023
M. Lackner and P. Skowron, *Multi-Winner Voting with Approval Preferences*,
SpringerBriefs in Intelligent Systems, https://doi.org/10.1007/978-3-031-09016-5_3

Table 3.1 Basic properties of ABC rules

	Pareto efficiency	Committee monoton.	Support monot. with add. voters	Support monot. without add. voters	Consist.	Inclusion-strategypr.	Comput. complexity
AV	Strong	✓	✓	✓	✓	✓	P
CC	Weak	×	✓	cand	✓	?	NP-hard
PAV	Strong	×	✓	cand	✓	×	NP-hard
seq-PAV	×	✓	cand	cand	×	×	P
seq-CC	×	✓	cand	cand	×	×	P
rev-seq-PAV	×	✓	✓	cand	×	×	P
Monroe	×	×	×	cand	×	×	NP-hard
Greedy Monroe	×	×	×	cand	×	×	P
seq-Phragmén	×	✓	cand	cand	×	×	P
leximax-Phragmén	×	×	cand	cand	×	?	NP-hard
Method of Eq. Shares	×	×	×	cand	×	×	P
MAV	Weak	×	✓	cand	×	×	NP-hard
SAV	Strong	✓	✓	✓	✓	×	P

it holds that $\mathcal{R}(A, k) = \mathcal{R}(\pi^* \circ A, k)$, where π^* is the natural extension of π to a bijection from $\mathcal{P}(C)$ to $\mathcal{P}(C)$ defined by $\pi^*(X) = \{\pi(c) : c \in X\}$ for each $X \subseteq C$. The rules that fail neutrality are usually those that require some form of tiebreaking.

The third and equally fundamental property we discuss here is resoluteness. Recall that an ABC rule is resolute if it always returns exactly one winning committee. An ABC rule can either be resolute or neutral, but not both. To see this, consider an approval profile where all voters approve candidates $\{a, b\}$ and $k = 1$: either a rule returns two winning committees or decides in favour of one of the two candidates. Clearly, any rule can be made resolute by imposing a tiebreaking between winning committees. Conversely, if a resolute rule is defined by a tiebreaking order over candidates (this includes all rules in Chap. 2 that fail neutrality), it can be made neutral by returning all committees that win according to *some* tiebreaking order. In this way, one can trade neutrality against resoluteness.

Finally, we mention that an in-depth treatment of the interplay between anonymity, neutrality, and resoluteness—albeit in the setting of single-winner elections—can be found in the work of Ozkes and Sanver [25] and Campbell and Kelly [5].

3.2 Pareto Efficiency and Condorcet Committees

Pareto efficiency[2] is a very general concept to compare two outcomes given the preferences of individuals: outcome Y dominates outcome X if (1) every individual weakly prefers outcome Y to X (i.e., everyone likes Y at least as much as X), and (2) there is at least one individual that strictly prefers Y to X. Pareto efficiency, broadly speaking, means that dominated outcomes are avoided. This concept can be directly translated to our setting by defining when a voter prefers committee W_1 to W_2. This requires a so-called *set extension*, i.e., a way how to extend preferences over individual items to sets of items; we refer the reader to the survey of Barberá et al. [4] for a comprehensive overview. Here, we use the Pareto efficiency definition by Lackner and Skowron [17] and assume that W_1 is preferred to W_2 if W_1 contains more approved candidates.

Definition 3.1 A committee W_1 dominates a committee W_2 if

1. every voter has at least as many approved candidates in W_1 as in W_2 (for $i \in N$ it holds that $|A(i) \cap W_1| \geq |A(i) \cap W_2|$), and
2. there is one voter with strictly more approved candidates (there exists $j \in N$ with $|A(j) \cap W_1| > |A(j) \cap W_2|$).

A committee that is not dominated by any other committee (of the same size) is called *Pareto optimal*.

An ABC rule $\mathcal{R}$ satisfies *strong Pareto efficiency* if $\mathcal{R}$ never outputs dominated committees. An ABC rule $\mathcal{R}$ satisfies *weak Pareto efficiency* if for all election instances (A, k) it holds that if $W_2 \in \mathcal{R}(A, k)$ and W_1 dominates W_2, then $W_1 \in \mathcal{R}(A, k)$.

Table 3.1 summaries which rules satisfy Pareto efficiency.[3] It may be surprising that rather few ABC rules satisfy this kind of Pareto efficiency. Indeed, among the rules introduced in Chap. 2 only Thiele rules, SAV, and MAV satisfy weak Pareto efficiency [17], and among those, e.g., AV, PAV, and SAV satisfy strong Pareto efficiency (but not CC and MAV, for details see Proposition A.1). (Although, we recall that these results rely of course on our chosen set extension.)

To see an example how a rule may fail Pareto efficiency, it is instructive to consider Monroe's rule:

Example 3.1 ([17, Example 3]) Consider the approval profile

$$2 \times \{a\} \quad 1 \times \{a, c\} \quad 1 \times \{a, d\} \quad 10 \times \{b, c\} \quad 10 \times \{b, d\}.$$

For $k = 2$, Monroe selects $\{c, d\}$ as the (only) winning committee with a Monroe-score of 22. Committee $\{c, d\}$ is however dominated by $\{a, b\}$: every voter approves

---

[2] Named after Vilfredo Pareto (1848–1923), an Italian economist [8].

[3] For details, in particular counterexamples, we refer the reader to [17]. Although this paper does not discuss the Method of Equal Shares, the counterexample for seq-Phragmén [17, Example 2] also works for this method.

a candidate in $\{a, b\}$ but only 22 voters approve one in $\{c, d\}$. Thus, every voter is either equally satisfied or better off with committee $\{a, b\}$. This example shows that Pareto efficiency clashes with Monroe's goal to assign representatives to groups of similar size.

One may wonder whether it is sensible to improve an ABC rule $\mathcal{R}$ that is not Pareto efficient in the following way: given an election instance E, if $W \in \mathcal{R}(E)$ is dominated by another committee, then instead output all Pareto optimal committees that dominate W. There are two main objections against this idea: First, this modification may destroy other axiomatic properties (e.g., Pareto efficiency and perfect representation, which is discussed in Sect. 4.3, are incompatible). Second, finding Pareto improvements is a computationally hard task:

Theorem 3.1 (Aziz and Monnot [3, Theorem 2]) *Given an election instance (A, k) and committee W, it is* coNP-*complete to determine whether W is Pareto optimal.*

As a consequence of Theorem 3.1, we cannot expect to obtain polynomial-time computable, Pareto efficient ABC rules by modifying existing rules as described above. Note, however, that polynomial-time computable, Pareto efficient ABC rules exist, e.g., AV and SAV. Thus, *finding* a Pareto optimal committee is possible in polynomial-time.

A related property to Pareto efficiency has been proposed by Darmann [6]: a committee W is a *Condorcet committee* if for every other committee W', for a majority of voters $V \subseteq N$ ($|V| > |N|/2$) it holds that $|A(i) \cap W| > |A(i) \cap W'|$ for all $i \in V$. Similarly to Theorem 3.1, deciding whether a given committee W is a Condorcet committee is coNP-complete. However, in contrast to Pareto optimality, it is also coNP-complete to decide whether a Condorcet committee exists [6]. To the best of our knowledge, it has not been analysed which ABC rules output a Condorcet committee if it exists.

3.3 Committee Monotonicity

Committee monotonicity (also referred to as house monotonicity or committee enlargement monotonicity) is a property that is highly desirable in some settings: if the committee size k is increased to $k + 1$, then a winning committee of size k should be a subset of a winning committee of size $k + 1$. Since this property is particularly useful for resolute rules, we define it exclusively for resolute rules. Appropriate definitions for irresolute rules can be found, e.g., in papers of Elkind et al. [9] and of Kilgour and Marshall [14] (called upward- and downward-accretive in the latter work).

Definition 3.2 A resolute ABC rule $\mathcal{R}$ is *committee monotone* if for all election instances (A, k) it holds that $W \subseteq W'$, where W is the single winning committee in $\mathcal{R}(A, k)$, and W' is the single winning committee in $\mathcal{R}(A, k + 1)$.

To see why committee monotonicity can be an essential requirement in some applications, consider the following situation. A group can jointly acquire k items and uses an ABC rule to fairly select those. Once these k items are purchased, it turns out that one additional item can be afforded. If the used ABC rule is committee monotone, it is clear which item to acquire next. However, if the rule is not committee monotone, then the selection for k + 1 items might contain several items that were not contained in the selection of k items, a useless recommendation.

Another example is a hiring process where it is not determined up-front how many candidates are to be hired. Here it is useful that a committee monotone rule actually produces a *ranking* of candidates: which one should be hired if only one position is available, which one if a second position is to be filled, etc. This connection between committee monotone ABC rules and rankings has been explored in-depth by Skowron et al. [32].

However, committee monotonicity also reduces the flexibility of voting rules and thus comes at a price. For example, we will see in Chap. 4 that committee monotone rules are typically less proportional (although a formal proof for this statement is missing). Thus, if the setting does not dictate committee monotonicity, it may be advantageous to set this axiom aside. A more elaborate discussion of this topic can be found in the paper of Elkind et al. [9].

Table 3.1 shows which of the considered rules are committee monotone, assuming that these rules are made resolute by fixing a tiebreaking order among candidates. AV, seq-PAV, seq-CC, rev-seq-PAV, seq-Phragmén, and SAV are committee monotone; this follows immediately from their corresponding definitions. Counterexamples for the remaining rules can be found in Appendix A, Proposition A.2.

3.4 Candidate and Support Monotonicity

Candidate monotonicity deals with a seemingly obvious requirement: if the support of a candidate increases (i.e., more voters approve this candidate), then this cannot harm the candidate's inclusion in a winning committee. However, this property is not satisfied by some ABC rules, in particular, if we demand such a monotonicity to also hold for groups of candidates. In addition, there is a difference depending on whether an existing voter changes her ballot, or if a new voter enters the election.

Candidate monotonicity axioms for ABC rules have been considered in a number of papers [2, 13, 16], but the paper by Sánchez-Fernández and Fisteus [27] should be highlighted for the most in-depth analysis.[4]

Further, we write A_{+X} to denote the profile A with one additional voter approving X, i.e., $A_{+X} = (A(1), \ldots, A(n), X)$, and A_{i+X} to denote the profile A where voter i additionally approves the candidates from X.

---

[4] Monotonicity is also studied in great detail by Elkind et al. [9] and Faliszewski et al. [10]; these works, however, largely focus on multi-winner voting with voters' preferences given as rankings (cf. Sect. 6.1).

Definition 3.3 (Sánchez-Fernández and Fisteus [27]) An ABC rule $\mathcal{R}$ satisfies *support monotonicity without additional voters* if for every election instance (A, k), $i \in N$, and candidate set $X \subseteq C$ it holds that

1. if $X \subseteq W$ for all $W \in \mathcal{R}(A, k)$, then $X \subseteq W'$ for all $W' \in \mathcal{R}(A_{i+X}, k)$, and
2. if $X \subseteq W$ for some $W \in \mathcal{R}(A, k)$, then $X \subseteq W'$ for some $W' \in \mathcal{R}(A_{i+X}, k)$.

An ABC rule $\mathcal{R}$ satisfies *support monotonicity with additional voters* if for any election instance (A, k) and candidate set $X \subseteq C$ the properties above hold for A_{+X} instead of A_{i+X}.

If an ABC rule satisfies these axioms only for singleton sets ($X = \{c\}$), we speak of *candidate monotonicity with/without additional voters*.[5]

The analysis of ABC rules with respect to these axioms is mostly due to Janson [13], Sánchez-Fernández and Fisteus [27], and Mora and Oliver [22]. We summarise the results in Table 3.1. There, the symbol ✓ means that support monotonicity is satisfied, "cand" means that candidate monotonicity is satisfied but not support monotonicity, and × means that the rule fails even candidate monotonicity. Detailed counterexamples related to support monotonicity can be found in Proposition A.3 in the appendix.

If one is interested in ABC rules that are—in a sense—fair to candidates, then candidate monotonicity (both with and without additional voters) is generally a desirable property. Hence, the fact that Monroe, Greedy Monroe, and the Method of Equal Shares fail the axiom can be seen as a serious argument against these rules. Monroe and the Method of Equal Shares, however, have other distinguished advantages (discussed in Chap. 4) that may override this downside. In settings where a fair treatment of candidates is not necessary (e.g., because candidates represent inanimate objects to be chosen), candidate monotonicity should not be a concern.

3.5 Consistency

Consistency is an axiom describing whether a rule behaves *consistently* with respect to disjoint groups: if the outcome of an election is the same for two disjoint groups, then a voting rule should arrive at this outcome also if these two groups are joined into a single electorate. This axiom is a straightforward adaption of consistency as defined for single-winner rules by Smith [34] and Young [36] and was first discussed in the context of ABC rules by Lackner and Skowron [18]. In the following, for two profiles A and A' we write $A + A'$ to denote the joint profile where A and A' are concatenated.

---

[5] Sánchez-Fernández and Fisteus [27] further introduce *weak support monotonicity with/without population increase*. These notions are slightly stronger than their candidate monotonicity counterparts (i.e., they imply candidate monotonicity with/without additional voters).

Definition 3.4 An ABC rule $\mathcal{R}$ satisfies *consistency* if for every $k \geq 1$ and two profiles $A : N \to \mathcal{P}(C)$ and $A' : N' \to \mathcal{P}(C)$ with $N \cap N' = \emptyset$, if $\mathcal{R}(A, k) \cap \mathcal{R}(A', k) \neq \emptyset$ then $\mathcal{R}(A + A', k) = \mathcal{R}(A, k) \cap \mathcal{R}(A', k)$.

Monroe's rule, for example, does not satisfy consistency:

Example 3.2 Let profile A be

$$A(1): \{a, y\} \quad A(2): \{a, y\} \quad A(3): \{b, y\} \quad A(4): \{b, y\}$$

and profile A' be

$$A(5): \{y\} \quad\quad A(6): \{a\} \quad\quad\quad A(7) = A(8) = A(9) = A(10): \{a, x\}$$
$$A(11): \{y\} \quad\quad A(12): \{b, y\} \quad\quad A(13) = A(14) = A(15) = A(16): \{b, x\}.$$

For $k = 2$, Monroe returns for profile A the winning committees $\{a, b\}$, $\{a, y\}$, and $\{b, y\}$, all of which having a Monroe-score of 4. For profile A', Monroe returns the winning committee $\{a, b\}$, with a Monroe-score of 10; the corresponding Monroe assignment groups voters 5–10 and 11–16. Now, let us consider the profile $A + A'$. Consistency would demand that $\{a, b\}$ is the unique winning committee, as it is the only committee winning in both A and A'. Committee $\{a, b\}$ has a Monroe-score of 14 in $A + A'$. This score, however, is not optimal: $\{x, y\}$ has a Monroe-score of 15; the corresponding Monroe assignment groups voters $\{1, \ldots, 6, 11, 12\}$ and $\{7, \ldots, 10, 13, \ldots, 16\}$. Thus, $\{a, b\}$ is not winning and consistency is violated.

Broadly speaking, the only rules satisfying consistency are so-called *ABC scoring rules* [18]. These are defined similarly to Thiele methods but are more general, as the satisfaction of a voter may depend on the number of candidates approved by this voter:

Definition 3.5 A *scoring function* is a function $f : \mathbb{N} \times \mathbb{N} \to \mathbb{R}$ satisfying $f(x, y) \geq f(x', y)$ for $x \geq x'$. Given such a scoring function, we define the score of W in A as

$$\text{score}_f(A, W) = \sum_{i \in N} f(|A(i) \cap W|, |A(i)|).$$

The *ABC scoring rule* defined by a scoring function f returns all committees with maximum score.

By definition, each Thiele method is an ABC scoring rule, whereas SAV is an example of an ABC scoring rule that is not a Thiele method. Further, it follows immediately from the definition of welfarist rules (Definition 2.1) that an ABC scoring rule is welfarist if and only if it is a Thiele method.

Lackner and Skowron [18] axiomatically characterised the class of ABC scoring rules. This characterisation is in a slightly different model than the one we use in this book: the characterisation applies to ABC ranking rules instead of ABC rules (as defined in Sect. 2.1). ABC ranking rules output a weak order over committees (a ranking with ties over committees) instead of just distinguishing between winning and losing committees (as we assume here). However, note that every ABC ranking rule defines an ABC rule (top-ranked committees are winning).

The following characterisation uses two axioms we have not mentioned so far: weak efficiency and continuity. Both are rather weak axioms. Intuitively, weak efficiency requires that approved candidates are preferable to non-approved candidates, and continuity states that a sufficiently large majority can force a committee to win.

Theorem 3.2 (Lackner and Skowron [18]) *An ABC ranking rule is an ABC scoring rule if and only if it satisfies anonymity, neutrality, consistency, weak efficiency, and continuity.*

As both weak efficiency and continuity are generally satisfied by sensible voting rules, one can conclude that ABC scoring rules essentially capture the class of consistent ABC ranking rules.[6] In Sect. 4.1, we will discuss how this result can be used to obtain further axiomatic characterisations, e.g., of PAV.

3.6 Strategic Voting

Strategic voting is a phenomenon central to social choice theory. Sometimes, it is preferable for voters to misrepresent their preferences to change the outcome of an election; this is often referred to as "manipulation". The famous impossibility theorem by Gibbard [12] and Satterthwaite [28], showing that all "reasonable" single-winner voting rules are susceptible to manipulation, is considered one of the main results in the field. The Gibbard–Satterthwaite theorem applies to elections where voters provide linear rankings over alternatives. As our approval-based setting uses a much more restricted form of preferences, strategyproofness is not completely out of the picture.

We are going to consider two forms of strategyproofness here: Cardinality-strategyproofness and inclusion-strategyproofness (taken from Peters [26], see the work of Gärdenfors [11] and Taylor [35] for more general discussions of strategyproofness in social choice). Cardinality-strategyproofness assumes that voters are concerned only about the number of approved candidates in the committee (and do not distinguish them), whereas inclusion-strategyproofness assumes that voters may have more complex preferences, so a successful manipulation must produce a committee including all approved candidates that were already included in the original committee.

---

[6] In the setting of single-winner rules a similar result holds: a social welfare function is a scoring rule if and only if it satisfies anonymity, neutrality, consistency, and continuity, as shown by Smith [34] and Young [36]. Moreover, a similar characterisation holds for committee scoring rules, as shown by Skowron et al. [33]. Committee scoring rules can be viewed as analogues of ABC scoring rules in the multi-winner model with preferences given as rankings (see Sect. 6.1); the proof of Theorem 3.2 builds upon this result.

To simplify the discussion, we assume resoluteness, i.e., we assume a (deterministic) tiebreaking order to resolve ties between committees. To clarify what it means that a voter misrepresents their true preferences, we use the concept of i-variants: Given profiles A and A', both with the same set of voters N, we say that A' is an i-variant of A if $A(j) = A'(j)$ for all $j \in N \setminus \{i\}$ with $j \neq i$. Let us first define both notions for resolute ABC rules.

Definition 3.6 A resolute ABC rule $\mathcal{R}$ satisfies *cardinality-strategyproofness* if for all profiles A and A' where A' is an i-variant of A and for all $k \geq 1$ it holds that $|\mathcal{R}(A, k) \cap A(i)| \geq |\mathcal{R}(A', k) \cap A(i)|$.

Definition 3.7 A resolute ABC rule $\mathcal{R}$ satisfies *inclusion-strategyproofness* if for all profiles A and A' where A' is an i-variant of A and for all $k \geq 1$ it holds that $\mathcal{R}(A, k) \cap A(i)$ is not a strict subset of $\mathcal{R}(A', k) \cap A(i)$.

Cardinality-strategyproofness is a stronger notion than inclusion-strategyproofness in the sense that all cardinality-strategyproof ABC rules are also inclusion-strategyproof. This follows from the fact that $|\mathcal{R}(A, k) \cap A(i)| \geq |\mathcal{R}(A', k) \cap A(i)|$ (as required in Definition 3.6) implies that $\mathcal{R}(A, k) \cap A(i)$ cannot be a strict subset of $\mathcal{R}(A', k) \cap A(i)$ (as required in Definition 3.7).

Among the rules considered in this book, only AV satisfies any of the mentioned strategyproofness axioms. Specifically, AV satisfies both inclusion-strategyproofness and cardinality-strategyproofness if AV is made resolute by any tiebreaking order on candidates (for details see Proposition A.4). None of the other ABC rules considered in this paper satisfy these axioms, see Table 3.1 for an overview and Proposition A.4 for details. However, even AV is not strategyproof in a stronger sense when voters have underlying, non-dichotomous preferences (as discussed, e.g., by Niemi [24]).

Both cardinality- and inclusion-strategyproofness can be generalised to irresolute ABC rules via set extensions, i.e., by defining how voters compare sets of committees. For example, Lackner and Skowron [16] propose a rather strong extension based on stochastic dominance. The resulting axiom, called SD-strategyproofness, implies cardinality-strategyproofness. AV satisfies SD-strategyproofness and can even be characterised in the class of ABC scoring rules (Definition 3.5) as the only rule satisfying SD-strategyproofness [16]. We note, however, that under more holistic models, e.g., models where voters have underlying non-dichotomous (non-binary) preferences, even AV is no longer strategyproof (see, e.g., [7, 19, 21, 31]). Another natural extension is the Kelly (or cautious) extension: a voter prefers $\mathcal{R}(A', k)$ to $\mathcal{R}(A, k)$ if every committee in $\mathcal{R}(A', k)$ is preferable to every committee in $\mathcal{R}(A, k)$. A more substantial discussion of strategyproofness of irresolute ABC rules can be found in the paper of Kluiving et al. [15].

We further discuss strategyproofness in Sect. 4.6 in the context of proportionality. We will see that even weak forms of proportionality are incompatible with strategyproofness.

Finally, we note that Scheuerman et al. [29, 30] have conducted a behavioural experiment in which they analysed how the voters vote under non-dichotomous preferences, when they are uncertain about other voters' preferences, and when AV is used to select the winning candidates. These results suggest that the voters may use different (sometimes suboptimal) heuristics when making decisions which candidates they should approve. This shows that strategic voting in a practical setting can differ substantially from the axiomatic analysis we have presented here.

References

1. K. J. Arrow. *Social Choice and Individual Values*. Wiley, New York, 2nd edition, 1963.
2. H. Aziz and B. E. Lee. The expanding approvals rule: Improving proportional representation and monotonicity. *Social Choice and Welfare*, 54(1):1–45, 2020.
3. H. Aziz and J. Monnot. Computing and testing Pareto optimal committees. *Autonomous Agents and Multi-Agent Systems*, 34(1):1–20, 2020.
4. S. Barberà, W. Bossert, and P. K. Pattanaik. Ranking sets of objects. In *Handbook of utility theory*, pages 893–977. Springer, 2004.
5. D. E. Campbell and J. S. Kelly. The finer structure of resolute, neutral, and anonymous social choice correspondences. *Economics Letters*, 132:109–111, 2015.
6. A. Darmann. How hard is it to tell which is a Condorcet committee? *Mathematical Social Sciences*, 66(3):282–292, 2013.
7. A. Dellis and M. P. Oak. Approval voting with endogenous candidates. *Games and Economic Behavior*, 54(1):47–76, 2006.
8. G. Eisermann. Pareto, Vilfredo (1848–1923). In *International Encyclopedia of the Social & Behavioral Sciences*, pages 11048–11051. Elsevier, 2001.
9. E. Elkind, P. Faliszewski, P. Skowron, and A. Slinko. Properties of multiwinner voting rules. *Social Choice and Welfare*, 48(3):599–632, 2017.
10. P. Faliszewski, P. Skowron, A. Slinko, and N. Talmon. Committee scoring rules: Axiomatic characterization and hierarchy. *ACM Transactions on Economics and Computation*, 6(1):Article 3, 2019.
11. P. Gärdenfors. On definitions of manipulation of social choice functions. In J.-J. Laffont, editor, *Aggregation and Revelation of Preferences*. North-Holland, 1979.
12. A. Gibbard. Manipulation of voting schemes. *Econometrica*, 41(4):587–601, 1973.
13. S. Janson. Phragmén's and Thiele's election methods. *CoRR*, abs/1611.08826, 2016. URL http://arxiv.org/abs/1611.08826.
14. D. M. Kilgour and E. Marshall. Approval balloting for fixed-size committees. In D. S. Felsenthal and M. Machover, editors, *Electoral Systems: Paradoxes, Assumptions, and Procedures*, Studies in Choice and Welfare, chapter 12, pages 305–326. Springer, 2012.
15. B. Kluiving, A. Vries, P. Vrijbergen, A. Boixel, and U. Endriss. Analysing irresolute multiwinner voting rules with approval ballots via SAT solving. In *Proceedings of the 24th European Conference on Artificial Intelligence (ECAI-2020)*, volume 325 of *Frontiers in Artificial Intelligence and Applications*, pages 131–138. IOS Press, 2020.
16. M. Lackner and P. Skowron. Approval-based multi-winner rules and strategic voting. In *Proceedings of the 27th International Joint Conference on Artificial Intelligence (IJCAI-2018)*, pages 340–436, 2018.
17. M. Lackner and P. Skowron. Utilitarian welfare and representation guarantees of approval-based multiwinner rules. *Artificial Intelligence*, 288:103366, 2020.
18. M. Lackner and P. Skowron. Consistent approval-based multi-winner rules. *Journal of Economic Theory*, 192:105173, 2021.
19. J.-F. Laslier and K. Van der Straeten. Strategic voting in multi-winners elections with approval balloting: a theory for large electorates. *Social Choice and Welfare*, 47(3):559–587, 2016.
20. K. O. May. A set of independent necessary and sufficient conditions for simple majority decision. *Econometrica*, 20(4):680–684, 1952.

21. R. Meir, A. D. Procaccia, J. S. Rosenschein, and A. Zohar. Complexity of strategic behavior in multi-winner elections. *Journal of Artificial Intelligence Research*, 33:149–178, 2008.
22. X. Mora and M. Oliver. Eleccions mitjançant el vot d'aprovació. El mètode de Phragmén i algunes variants. *Butlletí de la Societat Catalana de Matemàtiques*, 30(1):57–101, 2015.
23. H. Moulin. *Axioms of Cooperative Decision Making*. Cambridge University Press, 1988.
24. R. G. Niemi. The problem of strategic behavior under approval voting. *American Political Science Review*, 78(4):952–958, 1984.
25. A. I. Ozkes and M. R. Sanver. Anonymous, neutral, and resolute social choice revisited. *Social Choice and Welfare*, 57(1):97–113, 2021.
26. D. Peters. Proportionality and strategyproofness in multiwinner elections. In *Proceedings of the 17th International Conference on Autonomous Agents and Multiagent Systems (AAMAS-2018)*, pages 1549–1557, 2018.
27. L. Sánchez-Fernández and J. A. Fisteus. Monotonicity axioms in approval-based multi-winner voting rules. In *Proceedings of the 18th International Conference on Autonomous Agents and Multiagent Systems (AAMAS-2019)*, pages 485–493, 2019.
28. M. Satterthwaite. Strategy-proofness and Arrow's conditions: Existence and correspondence theorems for voting procedures and social welfare functions. *Journal of Economic Theory*, 10(2):187–217, 1975.
29. J. Scheuerman, J. Harman, N. Mattei, and K. B. Venable. Heuristic strategies in uncertain approval voting environments. In *Proceedings of the 19th International Conference on Autonomous Agents and Multiagent Systems (AAMAS-2020)*, pages 1993–1995, 2020.
30. J. Scheuerman, J. L. Harman, N. Mattei, and K. B. Venable. Modeling voters in multi-winner approval voting. In *Proceedings of the 35th Conference on Artificial Intelligence (AAAI-2021)*, pages 5709–5716, 2021.
31. F. D. Sinopoli, B. Dutta, and J.-F. Laslier. Approval voting: three examples. *International Journal of Game Theory*, 35(1):27–38, 2006.
32. P. Skowron, M. Lackner, M. Brill, D. Peters, and E. Elkind. Proportional rankings. In *Proceedings of the 26th International Joint Conference on Artificial Intelligence (IJCAI-2017)*, pages 409–415, 2017.
33. P. Skowron, P. Faliszewski, and A. Slinko. Axiomatic characterization of committee scoring rules. *Journal of Economic Theory*, 180:244–273, 2019.
34. J. Smith. Aggregation of preferences with variable electorate. *Econometrica*, 41(6):1027–1041, 1973.
35. A. D. Taylor. *Social choice and the mathematics of manipulation*. Cambridge University Press, 2005.
36. H. P. Young. A note on preference aggregation. *Econometrica*, 42(6):1129–1131, 1974.

Chapter 4
Proportionality

A key difference among ABC rules is how they treat minorities of voters, i.e., small groups with preferences different from larger groups. Let us illustrate this issue with the following simple example.

Example 4.1 Consider the approval-based preference profile with 60 voters approving $A = \{a_1, \ldots, a_{10}\}$, 20 voters approving $B = \{b_1, \ldots, b_6\}$, 10 voters approving $C = \{c_1, c_2\}$, 8 voters approving $D = \{d_1, d_2, d_3, d_4\}$, and 2 voters approving $E = \{e_1, e_2, e_3\}$; assume our goal is to pick a committee of ten candidates. Given this instance AV returns committee A, and in some cases this is a reasonable choice (e.g., when the goal of the election is to select finalists of a contest). Yet, when the goal is to select a representative body that should reflect voters' preferences in a proportional fashion, this committee violates very basic principles of fairness. Indeed, the voters who approve committee A constitute 60% of the population, yet effectively they decide about the whole committee; at the same time the group of 20% who approve B is ignored. A committee that consists of six candidates from A, two candidates from B, one candidate from C, and one candidate from D is, for example, a much more proportional choice.

In Example 4.1, picking an outcome that is intuitively proportional is easy due to a very specific structure of voters' approval sets—each two approval sets are either the same or disjoint. Finding a proportional committee in the general case, when any two approval sets can arbitrarily overlap, is by far less straightforward, and to some extent ambiguous. Several approaches that allow one to formally reason about proportionality have been proposed in the literature.

The goal of this chapter is to discuss the many faces of proportional representation. Proportionality, at its core, is a notion of fairness that grants smaller and larger groups of voters a fair consideration of their preferences.[1] The concrete definitions

---

[1] The concept of proportionality also finds application beyond voting, such as proportional clustering in machine learning [22, 49].

© The Author(s) 2023
M. Lackner and P. Skowron, *Multi-Winner Voting with Approval Preferences*,
SpringerBriefs in Intelligent Systems, https://doi.org/10.1007/978-3-031-09016-5_4

Table 4.1 Proportionality of ABC rule. There are three rules which perform particularly well in terms of proportionality: PAV, Phragmén's sequential rule, and the Method of Equal Shares. The mark † means that the result holds only when the number of voters n is divisible by the committee size k. References of the form (A.x) refer to propositions in Appendix A

	Proportionality degree	EJR	PJR	JR	Laminar prop.	Priceability	Apportionment
AV	0 [68]						None
PAV	$\ell - 1$ [4]	✓ [3]	✓ [3]	✓ [3]			D'Hondt [13]
seq-PAV	$\approx 0.7\ell - 1$ (for $k \leq 200$) [68]						D'Hondt [13]
rev-seq-PAV	?						D'Hondt [13]
CC	≤ 1 (Example 4.6)			✓ [3]			None
seq-CC	≤ 1 (Example 4.6)			✓ [3]			None
seq-Phragmén	$(\ell-1)/2$ [68]		✓ [12]	✓ [12]	✓ [56]	✓ [56]	D'Hondt [13]
M. Equal Shares	$(\ell\pm1)/2$ (A.10)	✓ [56]	✓ [56]	✓ [56]	✓ [56]	✓ [56]	D'Hondt [56]
leximax-Phragmén	1 [68]		✓ [12]	✓ [12]		✓ [56]	D'Hondt [13]
Monroe	≤ 1 (Ex. 4.6)		† [66]	✓ [3]			LRM † [13]
Greedy Monroe	≤ 1 (Ex. 4.6)		† [66]	✓ (A.7)			LRM † (A.5)
MAV	0 (A.10)						None
SAV	0 (A.10)						None

of what proportionality exactly means, however, differ. In this chapter, we review the main approaches to proportionality and identify ABC rules which can be considered proportional. Table 4.1 and Fig. 4.1 provide an overview of this analysis; the corresponding concepts are explained in this chapter.

But before we delve into this topic, let us answer the question why proportionality has such a prominent place in this book. The main reason is that this reflects the attention this topic has received. Since 2015, when Aziz et al. [3] first introduced (extended) justified representation (Sect. 4.2), there has been rapid progress in the understanding of proportionality in ABC elections. This progress has been along two trajectories: (i) defining stronger and stronger proportionality properties and (ii) finding (computationally tractable) ABC rules satisfying these properties. In many situations, a proportional committee corresponds to a fair selection of candidates. Thus, this line of research can be viewed as the search for a maximally fair ABC voting rule. The following sections (Sects. 4.1–4.4) provide an overview of this exciting endeavour.

However, non-proportional rules are certainly also relevant and even necessary in many applications. For example, when shortlisting candidates for a prize, we may want to select the "best" candidates without considerations of a proportional selection. Or if we want to form a group that deliberates a topic, we would like to

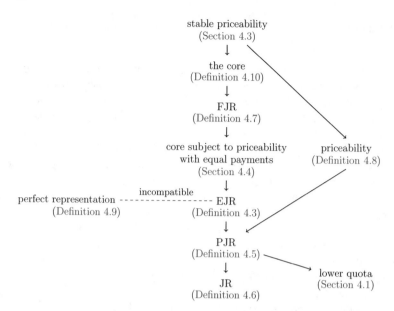

Fig. 4.1 The relation between different proportionality axioms. An arrow from property A to B means that A implies B

include as many diverse opinions as possible and thus we do not give a higher weight to popular opinions. In general, much less work has been done on analysing and understanding non-proportional rules and this topic deserves much more attention. In Sect. 4.5, we summarise the existing literature and discuss concepts of "non-proportionality".

The two final sections of this chapter are dedicated to the interplay of proportionality and strategyproofness (Sect. 4.7) and considerations of proportionality when candidates have external attributes (Sect. 4.6).

4.1 Apportionment

One approach to reasoning about proportionality of voting rules is to first identify a class of well-structured preference profiles where the concept of proportionality can be intuitively captured, and then to examine the behaviour of voting rules on such well-structured profiles. We focus here on so-called *party-list profiles*, which are election instances of the form as we have seen in Example 4.1.

Definition 4.1 (*Party-list profiles*) We say that an approval profile $A = (A(1), \ldots, A(n))$ is a *party-list profile* if for each two voters $i, j \in N$ we have that either $A(i) = A(j)$ or that $A(i) \cap A(j) = \emptyset$. We say that an election instance (A, k) is a *party-list instance* if (i) A is a party-list profile, and (ii) for each voter $i \in N$ we have that $|A(i)| \geq k$.

Party-list profiles closely resemble political elections with political parties, hence the name of the domain. In such elections, voters are typically asked to vote for exactly one party. To see the connection to party-list profiles, note the following: If A is a party-list profile, then the sets of voters and candidates can be divided into p disjoint groups each, $N = N_1 \cup \cdots \cup N_p$ and $C \supseteq C_1 \cup \cdots \cup C_p$, so that all voters from group $N_i, i \in [p]$, approve exactly the candidates from C_i (and no others). The candidates from C_i can be thought of as members of some (virtual) party, and the voters from N_i are those who cast their vote on party C_i.

In such elections, where the voters do not vote for individual candidates but rather each voter casts a single vote for one political party, the problem of distributing seats to political parties is called the *apportionment problem*. The concept of proportionality in the apportionment setting has been extensively studied in the literature and is well understood—for a detailed overview we refer the reader to the comprehensive books by Balinski and Young [5] and by Pukelsheim [62].

We see from Definition 4.1 that the apportionment problem can be viewed as a strict subdomain of approval-based multi-winner elections, and consequently ABC rules can be viewed as functions that extend apportionment methods to the more general setting of approval profiles. This connection was already known and referred to by Thiele [73] and Phragmén [59]. In a more systematic fashion, Brill et al. [13] showed such relations between various ABC rules and methods of apportionment. To properly explain this relation, let us first define three prominent apportionment methods, used in parliamentary elections all over the world.

In the following, we assume that there are p political parties, consisting of the candidate sets $C_1, \ldots, C_p$. By n_i we denote the number of votes cast on party C_i. Further, in line with our usual notation, k denotes the number of committee seats that we want to distribute among the parties.

Apportionment Rule 1 (D'Hondt method[2]) *The D'Hondt method proceeds in k rounds, in each round allocating one seat to some party. Consider the r-th round, and let $s_i(r)$ be the number of seats that are currently assigned to party C_i; thus, $\sum_{i \in [p]} s_i(r) = r - 1$. The D'Hondt method assigns the r-th seat to the party C_i with the highest ratio $\frac{n_i}{s_i(r)+1}$ (using a tiebreaking order between parties if necessary).*

---

[2] Victor D'Hondt (1841–1901) was a Belgian professor of law and active proponent of proportional representation [24, 25]. The D'Hondt method is also known as the Jefferson method. Thomas Jefferson (1743–1826) was president of the United States, and proposed this method to allocate seats in the House of Representatives to states. D'Hondt's proposal was specifically meant for proportional representation in parliaments. D'Hondt developed this method independently of Jefferson, even though Jefferson's proposal was earlier and largely similar. The name "Jefferson method" is typically used in the U.S., while "D'Hondt method" is prevalent in Europe.

Apportionment Rule 2 (Sainte-Laguë[3] method) *The Sainte-Laguë method is defined analogously to the D'Hondt method, but in the r-th round it allocates the r-th seat to the party C_i which maximises the ratio $\frac{n_i}{2s_i(r)+1}$.*

Both the D'Hondt and the Sainte-Laguë method belong to the class of divisor methods. Divisor methods differ in the formula for the ratio used to distribute seats to parties. The aforementioned books by Balinski and Young [5] and by Pukelsheim [62] discuss this important class of apportionment methods in much more detail.

Apportionment Rule 3 (Largest remainder method, LRM[4]) *The largest remainder method first assigns to each party $\lfloor k \cdot \frac{n_i}{n} \rfloor$ seats—this way at least $k - p + 1$ seats are assigned. Second, it assigns the remaining $r < p$ seats to the r parties with the largest remainders $k \cdot \frac{n_i}{n} - \lfloor k \cdot \frac{n_i}{n} \rfloor$, assigning each party at most one seat.*

Example 4.2 Consider a party-list representation of the profile from Example 4.1. We have five parties, A, B, C, D, and E, each getting, respectively, 60, 20, 10, 8, and 2 votes; the committee size is $k = 10$. The computation of the D'Hondt method can be followed in the left table below:

	A	B	C	D	E
n_i	**60**	**20**	**10**	8	2
$n_i/2$	**30**	**10**	5	4	1
$n_i/3$	**20**	6 2/3	3 1/3	2 2/3	2/3
$n_i/4$	**15**	5	2 1/2	2	1/2
$n_i/5$	**12**	4	2	1 3/5	2/5
$n_i/6$	**10**	3 1/3	1 2/3	1 1/3	1/3
$n_i/7$	**8 4/7**	2 6/7	1 3/7	1 1/7	2/7
$n_i/8$	7 1/2	2 1/2	1 1/4	1	1/4

	A	B	C	D	E
n_i	**60**	**20**	**10**	8	2
$n_i/3$	**20**	**6 2/3**	3 1/3	2 2/3	2/3
$n_i/5$	**12**	4	2	1 3/5	2/5
$n_i/7$	**8 4/7**	2 6/7	1 3/7	1 1/7	2/7
$n_i/9$	**6 2/3**	2 2/9	1 1/9	1 8/9	2/9
$n_i/11$	**5 5/11**	1 9/11	10/11	8/11	2/11
$n_i/13$	4 8/13	1 7/13	10/13	8/13	2/13
$n_i/15$	4	1 1/3	2/3	8/15	2/15

In the subsequent rounds the D'Hondt method allocates seats to parties A, A, A (by tie-breaking), B, A, A, A (by tie-breaking), B (by tie-breaking), C, and A. For example, in the fourth round, when A is already allocated 3 seats and B is allocated none, the rule will give the next seat to B rather than to A, because $\frac{20}{0+1} > \frac{60}{3+1}$. Summarising, seven seats will be allocated to party A, two seats to party B, and one seat to party C; the remaining parties will get no seats. In the diction of ABC rules, winning committees are exactly those that consist of seven candidates from A, two candidates from B and one candidate from C.

---

[3] As it is the case with the D'Hondt/Jefferson method, this rule has been developed independently in Europe and in the U.S. and goes by different names: Sainte-Laguë is used in Europe (in particular in the context of proportional representation in parliaments) and Webster is the name used in the U.S. literature. Sainte-Laguë (1882–1950) was a French mathematician and proposed this method in 1910 [65]. Daniel Webster (1782–1852) was a U.S. statesman and proposed this method in 1832 [5].

[4] The largest remainder method is also known as the Hamilton method, as it was proposed in the U.S. by Alexander Hamilton (1755–1804). His proposal was abandoned in favour of Jefferson's method [5].

The computation of the Sainte-Laguë method is illustrated in the above right table. It will allocate six seats to A, two seats to B, one seat to C, and one seat to D.

The largest remainder method first assigns to parties A, B, C, D, and E— respectively—6, 2, 1, 0, and 0 seats. Then, the remainders are considered:

	A	B	C	D	E
n_i	60	20	10	8	2
$\lfloor k \cdot \frac{n_i}{n} \rfloor$	6	2	1	0	0
Remainder	0	0	0	0.8	0.2
Seats	6	2	1	1	0

There is one unassigned seat which will be given to the party with the largest remainder, namely to D. Thus, LRM will allocate six seats to A, two seats to B, one seat to C, and one seat to D.

The D'Hondt method, the Sainte-Laguë method, and LRM exhibit particularly appealing properties. For example, the D'Hondt method satisfies *lower quota*, which means that a party i which receives n_i out of n votes must be allocated at least $\lfloor k \cdot n_i/n \rfloor$ committee seats. The largest remainder method satisfies not only lower quota but also *upper quota*: a party i with n_i out of n votes must not receive more than $\lceil k \cdot n_i/n \rceil$ seats. However, the largest remainder method fails an important axiom called population monotonicity, which states that an increase in support must not harm a party. In contrast, population monotonicity is satisfied by D'Hondt and Sainte-Laguë. For further details, we refer the interested reader to the aforementioned books on apportionment methods [5, 62].

We are now ready to formulate the main results of Brill et al. [13]:

Theorem 4.1 (Brill et al. [13]) *PAV, sequential PAV, seq-Phragmén, and leximax-Phragmén extend the D'Hondt method of apportionment. Phragmén's variance-minimising rule[5] extends the Sainte-Laguë method of apportionment. If n is divisible by k, then Monroe's rule extends the largest remainders method.*

Theorem 4.1 lists ABC rules that behave proportionally on party-list profiles and thus these rules can be considered good contenders for being proportional in the general ABC model. In addition, we show in the appendix that also Greedy Monroe extends the largest remainder method when n is divisible by k (Proposition A.5), but both Monroe's rule and Greedy Monroe do not if n is not divisible by k (Proposition A.6).

Lackner and Skowron [44] strengthened the results of Brill et al. [13], providing a strong argument in favour of PAV:

Theorem 4.2 (Lackner and Skowron [44]) *PAV is the unique extension of the D'Hondt method that satisfies neutrality, anonymity, consistency, and continuity.*

---

[5] This rule is similar to leximax-Phragmén but minimises the variance of loads instead of the maximum load, see [12, 36] for a precise definition.

Lackner and Skowron [44] further show that this result can be generalised to arbitrary divisor-based apportionment methods. For example, the Sainte-Laguë method yields the w-Thiele method with $w(x) = \sum_{j=1}^{x} \frac{1}{2j-1}$.

4.2 Cohesive Groups

In party-list profiles (Definition 4.1), voters can be arranged in groups with identical preferences. Then, proportionality requires that a large-enough group of voters with identical preferences deserves a certain number of representatives in the elected committee (proportional to the size of the group). This approach can be generalised to groups with non-identical but similar preferences. We now discuss axioms that relax the requirements for groups of voters to be entitled to representatives. These axioms are based on the concept of ℓ-cohesiveness:

Definition 4.2 For $\ell \geq 1$, a group $V \subseteq N$ is ℓ-*cohesive* if:

(i) $|V| \geq \ell \cdot \frac{n}{k}$, and
(ii) $\left| \bigcap_{i \in V} A(i) \right| \geq \ell$.

An ℓ-cohesive group consists of an ℓ/k-th fraction of voters, thus, intuitively, such a group should be able to control at least $\ell/k \cdot k = \ell$ committee seats. Further, an ℓ-cohesive group agrees on ℓ candidates, so one can ensure each member of the group gets ℓ representatives by selecting only ℓ candidates. It is, hence, tempting to require that for each ℓ-cohesive group V, each voter from V should be given at least ℓ representatives in the elected committee. Unfortunately, this would be too strong—there exists no rule that would satisfy this property.

Example 4.3 (Aziz et al. [4]) Consider a profile A with four candidates (a, b, c, d) and 12 voters, with the following approval sets:

$A(1): \{a, d\}$	$A(4): \{a, b\}$	$A(7): \{b, c\}$	$A(10): \{c, d\}$
$A(2): \{a\}$	$A(5): \{b\}$	$A(8): \{c\}$	$A(11): \{d\}$
$A(3): \{a\}$	$A(6): \{b\}$	$A(9): \{c\}$	$A(12): \{d\}.$

Let $k = 3$. The group $\{1, 2, 3, 4\}$ is 1-cohesive, as it has a commonly approved candidate (a) and is of size $\frac{12}{3} = 4$. If we want to give each voter in this group a representative, candidate a has to be in the winning committee (voters 2 and 3 only approve a). Now observe that also the groups $\{4, 5, 6, 7\}$, $\{7, 8, 9, 10\}$, and $\{10, 11, 12, 1\}$ are 1-cohesive. Thus, also candidates b, c, and d have to be in every winning committee. This is impossible as we are interested in committees of size 3. We see that it is impossible to satisfy *every* voter in 1-cohesive groups.

We see from this example that the requirement that each voter from an ℓ-cohesive group should have at least ℓ representatives in the elected committee is simply too strong.[6] However, it can be weakened a bit without losing much of its intuitive appeal. We start our discussion with *extended justified representation (EJR)* [3] and *proportionality degree* [4, 66, 68, 69].[7] The former concept is formulated as an axiom, the latter as a proportionality guarantee specified by a function.

Definition 4.3 (*Extended justified representation, EJR*) An ABC rule $\mathcal{R}$ satisfies *extended justified representation (EJR)* if for each election instance $E = (A, k)$, each winning committee $W \in \mathcal{R}(E)$, and each ℓ-cohesive group of voters V there exists a voter $i \in V$ with at least ℓ representatives in W, i.e., $|A(i) \cap W| \geq \ell$.

Example 4.4 Let us revisit Example 4.3. The committee $\{a, b, c\}$ satisfies the condition of EJR: every 1-cohesive group contains at least one voter with one representative in $\{a, b, c\}$. For example, for the 1-cohesive group $\{10, 11, 12, 1\}$, the voters 10 and 1 have a representative in the committee. Note that in this example actually all size-3 committees satisfy the EJR condition; also there are no ℓ-cohesive groups for $\ell \geq 2$.

Definition 4.4 (*Proportionality degree*) Fix a function $f \colon \mathbb{N} \to \mathbb{R}$. An ABC rule $\mathcal{R}$ has a *proportionality degree* of f if for each election instance $E = (A, k)$, each winning committee $W \in \mathcal{R}(E)$, and each ℓ-cohesive group of voters V, the average number of representatives that voters from V get in W is at least $f(\ell)$, i.e.,

$$\frac{1}{|V|} \cdot \sum_{i \in V} |A(i) \cap W| \geq f(\ell).$$

At first, it might appear that even for large cohesive groups, EJR gives a guarantee only to a single voter within this group. However, the EJR property applies to any group of agents: Let V be an ℓ-cohesive group. If we remove a voter with ℓ representatives (who, by EJR, is guaranteed to exist), the resulting group will be at least $(\ell - 1)$-cohesive. Consequently, in such a group there must exist a voter with at least $\ell - 1$ representatives, etc. As a consequence of this argument, EJR implies a proportionality degree of at least $f_{\mathcal{R}}(\ell) = \frac{\ell - 1}{2}$ [66]. The other direction does not hold: even an ABC rule with a proportionality degree of $f_{\mathcal{R}}(\ell) = \ell - 1$ may fail EJR (cf. Proposition A.8).

Example 4.3 also shows that there exists no rule with a proportionality degree of $f(\ell) = \ell$:

Example 4.5 Consider again the profile of Example 4.3. Assume, there exists a rule $\mathcal{R}$ with a proportionality degree of $f_{\mathcal{R}}(\ell) = \ell$ and let $k = 3$. The group $\{1, 2, 3, 4\}$ is 1-cohesive, so in order to ensure that these voters get on average one

---

[6] In a very recent work, Brill et al. [16] explore this intuitive (but unachievable) requirement—called individual representation—in much more depth. In particular, they show that all ABC rules presented in this book sometimes fail individual representation even for elections where such a committee exists. In addition, they study conditions under which individual representation can be satisfied.

[7] The concept of proportionality degree was initially referred to as *average satisfaction of ℓ-cohesive groups* [4, 66]. Skowron et al. [69] called an almost equivalent property κ-group representation.

representative, candidate a must be selected. By applying the same reasoning to $\{4, 5, 6, 7\}$ we infer that b must be selected. Analogously, we conclude that c and d must be selected. However, there are only three seats in the committee, a contradiction.

Aziz et al. [4] generalise the above example and prove that there exists no rule with a proportionality degree of $f(\ell) = \ell - 1 + \epsilon$ for $\epsilon > 0$. PAV matches this bound, and thus has an optimal proportionality degree. Below we include the proof of this result, since a similar idea is often used in the analysis of proportionality properties of Thiele methods.

Theorem 4.3 (Aziz et al. [3, 4]) *PAV has a proportionality degree of $\ell - 1$. It also satisfies EJR.*

Proof Consider an election $E = (A, k)$ and let W be a winning committee according to PAV. Let N and C denote the sets of voters and candidates in E, respectively. We will show that for each ℓ-cohesive group of voters V it holds that $\frac{1}{|V|} \cdot \sum_{i \in V} |A(i) \cap W| > \ell - 1$. This proves that PAV has the proportionality degree of $\ell - 1$. We can further conclude that there exists a voter $i \in V$ with $|A(i) \cap W| > \ell - 1$, and hence PAV also satisfies EJR.

Towards a contradiction assume there exists an ℓ-cohesive group of voters V with $\frac{1}{|V|} \cdot \sum_{i \in V} |A(i) \cap W| \leq \ell - 1$. We will show that there exists a pair of candidates, $c \in W$ and $c' \notin W$, such that $score_{PAV}(A, (W \cup \{c'\}) \setminus \{c\}) > score_{PAV}(A, W)$. This would indicate that we can replace one member of W with another not-selected candidate so that the new winning committee has a higher PAV-score than W. This would contradict the fact that W is a winning committee.

For convenience, for a set of candidates X and a candidate y we will use the notation:

$$\Delta(X, y) = score_{PAV}(X \cup \{y\}) - score_{PAV}(X),$$

i.e., $\Delta(X, y)$ is the marginal contribution of y given X.

Since $\frac{1}{|V|} \cdot \sum_{i \in V} |A(i) \cap W| \leq \ell - 1$ and V is ℓ-cohesive, there exists a not-selected candidate $c' \in C$ that is approved by all the voters from V. If we add this candidate to the committee W, the PAV-score will increase by:

$$\Delta(W, c') = \sum_{i \in N(c')} \frac{1}{|A(i) \cap W| + 1} \geq \sum_{i \in V} \frac{1}{|A(i) \cap W| + 1}.$$

From the inequality between the arithmetic and harmonic means we further get that:

$$\Delta(W, c') \geq \frac{|V|^2}{\sum_{i \in V} (|A(i) \cap W| + 1)} \geq \frac{|V|^2}{|V|(\ell - 1) + |V|} = \frac{|V|}{\ell} \geq \frac{n}{k}.$$

The last inequality follows from ℓ-cohesiveness.

Now, consider a committee $W' = W \cup \{c'\}$, and observe that

$$\sum_{c \in W'} \Delta(W' \setminus \{c\}, c) = \sum_{c \in W'} \sum_{i \in N(c)} \frac{1}{|A(i) \cap W'|} = \sum_{i \in N} \sum_{c \in A(i) \cap W'} \frac{1}{|A(i) \cap W'|}$$

$$= \sum_{i \in N: A(i) \cap W' \neq \emptyset} |A(i) \cap W'| \cdot \frac{1}{|A(i) \cap W'|} \leq n.$$

As a result, there exists $c \in W'$ such that $\Delta(W' \setminus \{c\}, c) \leq \frac{n}{k+1}$. Consequently:

$$\text{score}_{\text{PAV}}(A, (W \cup \{c'\}) \setminus \{c\}) = \text{score}_{\text{PAV}}(A, W) + \Delta(W, c') - \Delta(W' \setminus c, c)$$

$$\geq \text{score}_{\text{PAV}}(A, W) + \frac{n}{k} - \frac{n}{k+1} > \text{score}_{\text{PAV}}(A, W).$$

This yields a contradiction and completes the proof.   □

In contrast to PAV, the two sequential variants of PAV, seq-PAV and rev-seq-PAV, do not satisfy EJR. However, the proportionality guarantees of Theorem 4.3 also hold for a local-search variant of PAV [4], which—in contrast to PAV itself—runs in polynomial time. Thus, EJR and a proportionality degree of $\ell - 1$ are achievable in polynomial time. Aziz et al. [4] also construct a second polynomial-time computable (but rather involved) rule that satisfies EJR. More recently, Peters and Skowron [56] prove that the Method of Equal Shares, which is also computable in polynomial time, satisfies EJR. Among the rules introduced in Chap. 2, PAV and the Method of Equal Shares are the only ones that satisfy EJR. An overview of the proportionality degree of rules can be found in Table 4.1.

Let us now consider two properties that are weaker than EJR.

Definition 4.5 (*Proportional justified representation, PJR* [66]) An ABC rule $\mathcal{R}$ satisfies *proportional justified representation (PJR)* if for each election $E = (A, k)$, each winning committee $W \in \mathcal{R}(E)$, and each ℓ-cohesive group of voters V it holds that $\left| W \cap \left(\bigcup_{i \in V} A(i) \right) \right| \geq \ell$.

Definition 4.6 (*Justified representation, JR* [3]) An ABC rule $\mathcal{R}$ satisfies *justified representation (JR)* if for each election $E = (A, k)$, each $W \in \mathcal{R}(E)$, and each 1-cohesive group of voters V there exists a voter $i \in V$ who is represented by at least one member of W, i.e., $|W \cap A(i)| \geq 1$.

PJR and JR are much weaker properties than EJR; in particular EJR implies PJR, which in turn implies JR. Example 4.6, below, illustrates that the stronger of the two axioms, PJR, can be satisfied even by rules that could be considered very bad from the perspective of proportionality degree (and, thus, also from the perspective of approximating EJR). On the other hand, there exist rules with good proportionality degree that do not satisfy even JR—this happens, e.g., when a rule does not provide sufficient guarantees for 1-cohesive groups (although it might satisfy EJR for $\ell \geq 2$). Generally, justified representation cannot be viewed as a proportionality axiom as it grants even large group only a single representative in the selected committee. In contrast, PJR can be viewed as a moderate proportionality requirement, significantly weaker than EJR but stronger than, e.g., lower quota on party-list profile. We refer to Table 4.1 for an overview which rules satisfy JR and PJR.

Example 4.6 Fix k and consider the following instance:

		c_{2k}			
		$\cdots$			
		c_{k+2}			
		c_{k+1}			
c_1	c_2	c_3		$\cdots$	c_k
V_1	V_2	V_3		$\cdots$	V_k

There are $2k$ candidates. The voters can be divided into k equal-size groups so that the voters from the ith group, in the diagram denoted as V_i, approve c_i and $\{c_{k+1}, \ldots, c_{2k}\}$. Committee $\{c_1, \ldots, c_k\}$ (marked blue) satisfies PJR, but clearly, $\{c_{k+1}, \ldots, c_{2k}\}$ (marked green) is a much better choice from the perspective of proportionality degree. Also, $\{c_{k+1}, \ldots, c_{2k}\}$ satisfies the EJR condition while $\{c_1, \ldots, c_k\}$ does not. This example shows that PJR implies no better proportionality degree than $f(\ell) = 1$.

Given that there are rather few rules satisfying EJR, Bredereck et al. [11] performed computer simulations for several distributions of voters' preferences and verified how hard it is *on average* to find a committee that satisfies the condition imposed by EJR. They concluded that ℓ-cohesive groups for $\ell \geq 2$ are quite rare, and that a random committee among those that satisfy the much weaker condition of JR is quite likely to satisfy EJR as well. Their second conclusion was that JR, PJR, and EJR, while highly desired, do not guarantee on their own a sensible selection of committees, and one needs to put forward additional criteria. Specifically, they showed that there are often many committees satisfying these conditions, and these committees may vary significantly. Bredereck et al. [11] derived their conclusions from the analysis of specific distributions of voters' preferences; it would be desirable to analyse this phenomenon more broadly, e.g., for other types of distributions.

Recently, Peters et al. [57] introduced an even stronger axiom, called *fully justified representation (FJR)*, where the precondition of ℓ-cohesiveness is relaxed. In EJR we say that a group of voters V is ℓ-cohesive if $|V| \geq \ell \cdot {}^n/_k$ and if there exists a set T of ℓ candidates such that each voter from V approves all ℓ candidates from T. In the definition of FJR, on the other hand, we only require that there must exist an integer β such that each voter from V approves at least β candidates from T. FJR enforces that at least one member of V must have at least β representatives in the elected committee. Note that EJR corresponds to FJR with a fixed value of $\beta = \ell$.

Definition 4.7 (*Fully justified representation* [57]) Given an integer value β and a subset of candidates $T \subseteq C$, we say that a group of voters V is weakly (β, T)-cohesive if $|V| \geq |T| \cdot n/k$ and if for each voter $i \in V$ it holds that $|A(i) \cap T| \geq \beta$. An ABC rule $\mathcal{R}$ satisfies *fully justified representation (FJR)* if for each election $E = (A, k)$, each winning committee $W \in \mathcal{R}(E)$, each integer β and $T \subseteq C$, and each weakly (β, T)-cohesive group of voters V, there exists a voter $i \in V$ such that $|W \cap A(i)| \geq \beta$.

For the time being, the only known rule that satisfies FJR is rather artificial and specifically tailored to the definition of the axiom [57]. It is an open question whether there exists a natural ABC rule which satisfies FJR together with other desirable properties.

All proportionality concepts discussed in this section ensure that cohesive groups are guaranteed a certain representation in the elected committee. Cevallos and Stewart [19] argue that in some contexts—for example when using ABC rules for selecting validators in the blockchain protocol—it is equally important to ensure that groups are not over-represented. To the best of our knowledge formal axioms capturing this intuitive requirement are still missing.[8]

To sum up, when considering proportionality axioms based on cohesive groups, PAV stands out as the most proportional rule. The Method of Equal Shares comes at a close second (its proportionality degree is lower) but it is computable in polynomial time. If we desire a committee monotone rule, then seq-Phragmén is a very good choice: it has a proportionality degree of $f_{\text{Phrag}}(\ell) = \frac{\ell-1}{2}$ [68], i.e., the proportionality degree that is implied by EJR, and satisfies PJR [12]. Also seq-PAV is a good choice: for reasonable sizes of committees seq-PAV has a better proportionality degree than seq-Phragmén; on the other hand, it satisfies neither PJR nor JR.

4.3   Laminar Proportionality and Priceability

The properties that we discussed in Sect. 4.2 (extended justified representation and the proportionality degree) and the axiomatic characterisation given in Theorem 4.2 all indicate that PAV provides particularly strong proportionality guarantees. Specifically, one could interpret these results as suggesting that PAV is a better rule—in terms of proportionality—than Phragmén's sequential rule and the Method of Equal Shares. However, drawing such a conclusion based on the so-far presented results would be too early. In the following we explain that proportionality can be understood in at least two different ways and that the axioms we discussed so far capture and formalise only one specific form of proportionality. We explain that Phragmén's sequential rule and the Method of Equal Shares provide very strong proportionality guarantees, but with respect to an interpretation of proportionality that is not captured by properties based on cohesive groups, and which is—to some extent—incomparable with the type of proportionality guaranteed by PAV.

---

[8] We note that the upper quota axiom in the apportionment setting can be viewed as such an axiom.

Let us start by illustrating the difference in how PAV and Phragmén's sequential rule (and the Method of Equal Shares) operate with the following example.

Example 4.7 ([56]) There are 15 candidates and 6 voters—the voters' approval sets are depicted in the diagram below. The committee shaded in blue in the left-hand side picture is the one that is selected by the Phragmén's sequential rule and by the Method of Equal Shares. The committee shaded in the right-hand side picture is chosen by PAV.

c_4	c_5	c_6			
c_3			c_9	c_{12}	c_{15}
c_2			c_8	c_{11}	c_{14}
c_1			c_7	c_{10}	c_{13}
1	2	3	4	5	6

(a) seq-Phragmén and Equal Shares

c_4	c_5	c_6			
c_3			c_9	c_{12}	c_{15}
c_2			c_8	c_{11}	c_{14}
c_1			c_7	c_{10}	c_{13}
1	2	3	4	5	6

(b) PAV

The approval sets of voters 1, 2, and 3 are disjoint from those of voters 4, 5, and 6. It seems intuitive that the first three voters, who together form half of the society, should be able to decide about half of the elected candidates. Phragmén's sequential rule and the Method of Equal Shares select committees where the first three voters approve in total half of the members, thus the behaviour of these rules is consistent with the aforementioned understanding of proportionality. PAV follows a different principle: In the committee depicted in (a), each of the first three voters approves 4 candidates; each of the remaining three voters approves only 2 committee members. PAV notices that this is the case, and tries to reduce the societal inequality of voters' satisfaction by removing one representative of voter 1 and adding one to 4; similarly, PAV considers that it is more fair to remove the representatives of 2 and 3, and add the candidates liked by 5 and 6. On the one hand, PAV prefers to pick a committee that minimises the societal inequality in the voters' satisfactions (measured as the number of approved committee members). On the other hand, it punishes voters 1, 2, and 3 for being agreeable and "easy to satisfy" with fewer committee members—PAV allows them to decide only about one quarter of the committee.

Example 4.7 illustrates that PAV and Phragmén's sequential rule (and the Method of Equal Shares) follow two different types of proportionality. PAV implements a *welfarist* type of proportionality which is primarily concerned with the welfare (satisfaction) of the voters. This type of proportionality is captured, e.g., by the properties discussed in Sect. 4.2. PAV also satisfies the Pigou–Dalton principle of transfers, which says that given an election (A, k) and two committees, W and W', which in total get the same numbers of approvals ($\text{score}_{AV}(A, W) = \text{score}_{AV}(A, W')$), the one which minimises the societal inequality should be preferred [56]. Phragmén's sequential rule and the Method of Equal Shares, on the other hand, implement proportionality with respect to power, which—informally speaking—says that a group consisting of an α fraction of voters should be given a voting power that enables to decide about an α fraction of the committee. In other words, the type of proportionality of Phragmén-like rules is not mainly concerned with the welfare of groups but with the justification of welfare, achieved by endowing each voter with the same amount of virtual budget that represents the voting power.

Peters and Skowron [56] discuss two properties—laminar proportionality and priceability—which aim at formally capturing the high-level idea of proportionality with respect to power.[9] The first of the two properties—*laminar proportionality*— is very similar in spirit to proportionality on party-list profiles. The corresponding axiom identifies a class of well-structured election instances—called *laminar elections*—and specifies how a laminar proportional rule should behave on these profiles. Laminar profiles are more general than party-list profiles and are defined by a recursive structure, similar to the election from Example 4.7.

The second property, which we will discuss in more detail, is *priceability*. Intuitively, we say that a committee W is priceable if we can endow each voter with the same fixed budget and if for each voter there exists a payment function such that: (1) voters do not spend more than their allotted budget, (2) voters pay only for the candidates they approve, (3) each elected candidate gets a total payment of 1; candidates that are not elected receive no payments, and (4) there is no group of voters who approve a non-elected candidate, and who in total have more than one unit of unspent budget. Priceability is a notion of proportionality as it distributes power to groups of sufficient size; a large enough group receives enough collective budget to afford one or more candidates in the committee.

Formally, we obtain the following definition:

Definition 4.8 (*Priceability*) Given an election instance (A, k), a committee W is priceable if there exists a per-voter budget $p \in \mathbb{R}_+$ and $p_i : C \to [0, 1]$ for each voter $i \in N$ such that:

(1) $\sum_{c \in C} p_i(c) \leq p$ for each $i \in N$,

(2) $p_i(c) = 0$ for each $i \in N$ and $c \notin A(i)$,

(3) $\sum_{i \in N} p_i(c) = \begin{cases} 1 & \text{if } c \in W, \\ 0 & \text{otherwise.} \end{cases}$

(4) $\sum_{i \in N(c)} \left(p - \sum_{c' \in W} p_i(c') \right) \leq 1$ for each $c \notin W$.

An ABC rule is priceable if it returns only priceable committees.

Example 4.8 Consider the election instance from Example 4.7. The committees returned by Phragmén's sequential rule and by the Method of Equal Shares are priceable. For example, consider $W_1 = \{c_1, \ldots, c_6, c_7, c_8, c_{10}, c_{11}, c_{13}, c_{14}\}$ (the committee shaded blue in the left figure in Example 4.7). This committee is priceable as witnessed by the following price system: the voters' budget is $p = 2$, and the payment functions are as follows (we only specify the non-zero payments): $p_1(c_i) = p_2(c_i) =$

---

[9] Laminar proportionality and priceability are similar in spirit but are logically independent (neither implies the other).

$p_3(c_i) = 1/3$ for $i \in \{1, 2, 3\}$ and $p_1(c_4) = p_2(c_5) = p_3(c_6) = p_4(c_7) = p_4(c_8) = p_5(c_{10}) = p_5(c_{11}) = p_6(c_{13}) = p_6(c_{14}) = 1$. Each voter fully spends their budget of 2.

On the other hand, the committee $W_2 = \{c_1, c_2, c_3, c_7, \ldots, c_{15}\}$ returned by PAV (the one shaded blue in the right figure in Example 4.7) is not priceable. Indeed, if the voters' budget p were ≤ 2, then the voters 4, 5, 6 could not afford to pay for 9 candidates $c_7, \ldots, c_{15}$. If $p > 2$, then some of the voters 1, 2, 3, say voter 1, would have a remaining budget of more than 1. Hence, this voter would have more budget than needed to buy a candidate outside of W_2 (e.g., c_4), which contradicts condition (4) in Definition 4.8.

Peters and Skowron [56] generalised Example 4.8 and showed that no welfarist rule (see Definition 2.1) is priceable. This shows that priceability is inherently not a welfarist concept. The same is true for laminar proportionality.

Theorem 4.4 (Peters and Skowron [56]) *Phragmén's sequential rule and the Method of Equal Shares are laminar proportional and priceable. No welfarist rule is laminar proportional nor priceable. No rule satisfying the Pigou–Dalton principle of transfers is laminar proportional nor priceable.*

While priceability is not a welfarist concept, it implies proportional justified representation. Further, all priceable rules must be equivalent to the D'Hondt method of apportionment on party-list profiles (cf. Theorem 4.1). A price system provides an explicit and easily verifiable evidence explaining that the voters can use their power (represented through virtual money) to ensure that the candidates from the committee are selected. This intuitively explains that priceability captures the idea of proportionality with respect to power—proportionality follows from the fact that each voter is initially endowed with the same amount of virtual money.

Priceability itself puts rather mild constraints on the payment functions $\{p_i\}_{i \in N}$. Recently, Peters et al. [58] introduced a stronger version of the axiom: we say that a price system $(p, \{p_i\}_{i \in N})$ is *stable* if it satisfies conditions (1)–(3) from Definition 4.8 and the following strengthening of condition (4):

(4*) Condition for Stability: There exists no non-empty group of voters $V \subseteq N$, no subset $W' \subseteq C \setminus W$, and no collections $\{p'_i\}_{i \in V}$ ($p'_i : W' \to [0, 1]$) and $\{R_i\}_{i \in V}$ (with $R_i \subseteq W$ for all $i \in V$) such that all the following conditions hold:

1. For each $c \in W'$: $\sum_{i \in V} p'_i(c) > 1$.
2. For each $i \in V$: $p_i(W \setminus R_i) + p'_i(W') \leq p$.
3. Each voter $i \in V$ approves more candidates in $W \setminus R_i \cup W'$ than in W, or i approves as many candidates in $W \setminus R_i \cup W'$ as in W but $\sum_{c \in W \setminus R_i} p_i(c) + \sum_{c \in W'} p'_i(c) < \sum_{c \in W} p_i(c)$.

In words, it should not be possible for the voters from V to propose a set of candidates W' such that if each voter $i \in V$ transferred her money from $R_i \subseteq W$ to the candidates from W', then these candidates would garner more than enough money to be elected, and each voter from $i \in V$ would be happier with $W \setminus R_i \cup W'$ than with W.

Stable priceability is a strong condition: stable-priceable committees do not always exist, and if so, they belong to the core (see Sect. 4.4). On the other hand, one can check in a polynomial time whether a committee is stable-priceable, and such committees often exist in practice. Peters et al. [58] also introduced the concept of *balanced stable-priceability*, which additionally requires that each two voters must pay the same amount of virtual money for the same candidate. They proved that balanced stable-priceable committees can be characterised as outputs of slightly modified version of the Method of Equal Shares.

We mention one more property—*perfect representation* [66]—which is loosely related to priceability. It also requires an explanation how voters can distribute their support/power in a way that justifies electing a committee; however, the axiom applies only in very specific situations.

Definition 4.9 (Sánchez-Fernández et al. [66]) We say that a committee W satisfies *perfect representation* if the set of voters can be divided into k equally-sized disjoint groups $N = N_1 \cup \ldots \cup N_k$ ($|N_i| = n/k$ for each $i \in k$) and if we can assign a distinct candidate from W to each of these groups in a way that for each $i \in k$ the voters from N_i all approve their assigned candidate. An ABC rule $\mathcal{R}$ satisfies perfect representation if $\mathcal{R}$ returns only committees satisfying perfect representation whenever such committees exist.

Perfect representation is incompatible with EJR [66] and with weak (and strong) Pareto efficiency (Proposition A.9), and it is not implied by (nor implies) priceability. Among the rules considered in this paper, only Monroe [66] and leximax-Phragmén [12] satisfy perfect representation, as does the variance-based rule by Phragmén mentioned in Theorem 4.1 [12].

To sum up, if we are mainly interested in the welfarist interpretation of proportionality, as captured by axioms that specify how cohesive groups of voters should be treated, then PAV is the best among the considered rules. Yet, sequential PAV, seq-Phragmén, and the Method of Equal Shares perform also reasonably well with respect to these criteria, and they are computable in polynomial time. Sequential PAV does not satisfy JR, and so it might discriminate small cohesive groups of voters. On the other hand, for reasonably small committees sequential PAV has better proportionality degree than seq-Phragmén, and the Method of Equal Shares. The axioms that well describe the welfarist type of proportionality are EJR and proportionality degree, and to a lesser extent PJR and JR. If we are interested in proportionality with respect to power, then we shall also consider the axioms of priceability and laminar proportionality. In this case the Method of Equal Shares and Phragmén's sequential rule are the two superior rules. It is not entirely clear which one of the two rules is better. On the one hand, the Method of Equal Shares satisfies the appealing axiom of EJR; on the other hand, Phragmén's sequential rule is committee monotone (see Sect. 3.3). In Table 4.1, we highlighted the three rules that—with the current state of knowledge—we consider the best ABC rules in terms of proportionality.

4.4 The Core

An important concept of group fairness that has been extensively studied in the context of ABC rules is the *core*. This notion of proportionality is adopted from cooperative game theory,[10] and was first introduced in the context of multi-winner voting by Aziz et al. [3].

Definition 4.10 Given an instance (A, k) we say that a committee W is in the *core* if for each non-empty $V \subseteq N$ and each $T \subseteq C$ with

$$\frac{|T|}{k} \le \frac{|V|}{n}, \tag{4.1}$$

there exists a voter $i \in V$ such that $|A(i) \cap T| \le |A(i) \cap W|$, i.e., voter i is at least as satisfied with W as with T. We say that an ABC rule $\mathcal{R}$ satisfies the core property if for each instance (A, k) each winning committee $W \in \mathcal{R}(A, k)$ is in the core.

Informally speaking, the core property requires that a group V constituting an α fraction of voters should be able to control an α fraction of the committee. If such a group can propose a set T of $\lfloor \alpha k \rfloor$ candidates such that each voter in V is more satisfied with the proposed set T than with the winning committee W, then the group V would have an incentive to deviate, hence would witness that committee W is not stable (and, in some sense, also not fair). If a winning committee is in the core, then no such deviation is possible.

The core property implies extended justified representation (Definition 4.3): Assume an ABC rule $\mathcal{R}$ satisfies the core property and consider an instance (A, k), a winning committee W, and an ℓ-cohesive group of voters V. Let T be the set of ℓ candidates that are approved by all the voters in V (such candidates exist because V is ℓ-cohesive). Since W is in the core, there must exist a voter $i \in V$ such that $|A(i) \cap W| \ge |A(i) \cap T| = \ell$, hence the condition of EJR must be satisfied. While the notion of core strictly generalises EJR and thus implies strong satisfaction guarantees for cohesive groups, it can also be viewed as a concept formalising the idea of proportionality with respect to power (cf. Sect. 4.3).

It is an important open question whether there exists an ABC rule that satisfies the core property, or—equivalently—whether the core is always non-empty. For the time being only partial answers to this intriguing question are known:

1. None of the rules mentioned in Chap. 2 satisfies the property. Since a rule satisfying the core must satisfy EJR, only PAV and the Method of Equal Shares come into consideration. However, counterexamples for both are known [3, 56]. For PAV, the instance from Example 4.7 shows a violation of the core. A simple example for the Method of Equal Shares can be found in [60, Example 4].
2. No welfarist rule (Definition 2.1) can satisfy the core property [56].

---

[10] Specifically, the definition used in the literature on multi-winner voting is based on the definition of the core for cooperative games with non-transferable payoffs [20, 52].

3. If one restricts the attention to a special subclass of approval profiles, so-called *approval-based party-list profiles* as introduced by Brill et al. [15], the situation changes. Approval-based party-list profiles are approval profiles where each candidate appears with at least k copies, i.e., for every candidate c it holds that $\left|\{c' \in C : N(c) = N(c')\}\right| \geq k$. Approval-based party-list profiles are thus *more general* than party-list profiles (cf. Definition 4.1)—intuitively each voter can approve one or more parties. Brill et al. [15] prove that PAV satisfies the core property on approval-based party-list profiles. As mentioned before, PAV does not satisfy the core property in the general case.
4. It is known that the core can be empty in settings that are related to the ABC model but are more expressive. This is the case, e.g., in committee elections with ranking-based preferences [23, 60] and in participatory budgeting with additive utilities [30, Appendix C]; these two settings are discussed Sect. 6.1 and in Sect. 6.4, respectively.

As it remains unclear whether an ABC rule satisfying the core property is an achievable goal, several works in the most recent literature analysed relaxed notions of the core. We review these notions in the following.

4.4.1 Relaxation by Randomisation

The first type of relaxation that we consider is a probabilistic variant of the notion, i.e., the question becomes: "can core-like properties be guaranteed in expectation (exante)?" Cheng et al. [23] prove that there always exists a lottery over committees that satisfies the core property in expectation. Let $\mathbb{E}_{X \sim \Delta}(X)$ denote the expected value of a random variable X distributed according to a lottery (probability distribution) Δ.

Theorem 4.5 (Cheng et al. [23]) *For each election instance (A, k) there exists a lottery over committees Δ such that for each group of candidates $T \subseteq C$ it holds that*

$$\frac{|T|}{k} > \frac{\mathbb{E}_{W \sim \Delta}(N(T, W))}{n}, \tag{4.2}$$

where $N(T, W)$ is the set of voters who prefer T over W:

$$N(T, W) = \{i \in N : |A(i) \cap T| > |A(i) \cap W|\}.$$

Note that Eq. (4.2) is indeed a negated, probabilistic version of Eq. (4.1), showing that in expectation there are too few voters to propose a different committee. While it is not known whether such a lottery Δ can be found in a polynomial time, Cheng et al. [23] prove that if we restrict our attention only to sets T of size bounded by a constant, then for each $\epsilon > 0$ there is a polynomial-time algorithm that computes Δ such that $(1 + \epsilon) \cdot \frac{|T|}{k} > \frac{\mathbb{E}_{W \sim \Delta}(N(T,W))}{n}$.

4.4.2 Relaxation by Deterministic Approximation

Another approach is to ask whether the core property can be well approximated. A few notions of approximation have been proposed; Definition 4.11 below unifies the definitions considered in the literature.

Definition 4.11 We say that an ABC rule $\mathcal{R}$ provides a γ-multiplicative-η-additive-satisfaction β-group-size approximation to the core if for each instance (A, k), each winning committee $W \in \mathcal{R}(A, k)$, each non-empty subset of voters $V \subseteq N$, and each subset of candidates $T \subseteq C$ with

$$\beta \cdot \frac{|T|}{k} \leq \frac{|V|}{n}$$

there exists a voter $i \in V$ such that $|A(i) \cap T| \leq \gamma \cdot |A(i) \cap W| + \eta$.

There are two components in Definition 4.11: The satisfaction-approximation component says that a voter i has an incentive to deviate towards T only if her gain in satisfaction is sufficiently large, that is, if i's satisfaction in T is greater at least by a multiplicative factor of γ *and* an additive factor of η than her satisfaction in W. The group-size-approximation component prohibits deviations towards sets T which are (by a multiplicative factor of β) smaller than $k \cdot \frac{|V|}{n}$, as imposed by the core. If $\gamma = 1$, then we omit the term "γ-multiplicative" from the name of the property. Similarly, if $\eta = 0$ we omit the term "η-additive", and if $\beta = 1$, then we omit the term "β-group-size". The satisfaction-approximation and the group-size approximation are incomparable.

When considering the problem of approximating the core, we distinguish two classes of algorithms. The first class contains dedicated approximation algorithms, which are mostly based on dependent rounding of fractional committees. The second class consists of established rules, such as PAV or the Method of Equal Shares, which can be shown to approximate the core (to some degree).

Jiang et al. [38] present an algorithm that provides 32-group-size approximation to the core. Their approach is based on dependent rounding of lotteries that are in expectation in the core (the existence of such lotteries is guaranteed by Theorem 4.5). Notably, the approach of Jiang et al. [38] extends much beyond the approval-based preferences; for cardinal utilities they round a lottery that in expectation 2-approximates the core and obtain a discrete committee with the 32-group-size approximation guarantee.

Fain et al. [30] present a family of algorithms based on dependent rounding of fractional committees (returned by a linear program that closely resembles the formulation of PAV as an integer linear program). For each $\lambda \in (1, 2]$ they provide an algorithm that guarantees a λ-multiplicative-η-additive-satisfaction $\frac{1}{2-\lambda}$-group-size approximation to the core, where $\eta = O\left(\frac{1}{\lambda^4} \log\left(\frac{k}{\lambda}\right)\right)$. Their algorithm naturally extends to a more general model related to participatory budgeting.

The result of Fain et al. [30] has recently been improved. Munagala et al. [51] presented a polynomial time algorithm that guarantees 67.37-multiplicative-1-additive-satisfaction approximation to the core. They also presented an algorithm that offers a 9.27-multiplicative-1-additive-satisfaction approximation to the core, yet running in exponential time. These algorithms, which are based on dependent rounding, can be also applied to more general types of voters' preferences.

For commonly known rules the following results are known: Cheng et al. [23] prove that PAV does not guarantee β-group-size approximation to the core even for $\beta = \Theta(\sqrt{k})$. On the other hand, Peters and Skowron [56] prove that PAV gives 2-multiplicative-satisfaction approximation to the core. Further, for each $\epsilon > 0$ no rule that satisfies the Pigou–Dalton principle can provide a $(2 - \epsilon)$-multiplicative-satisfaction approximation to the core. Thus, PAV can be viewed as giving the strongest multiplicative-satisfaction approximation to the core subject to satisfying the Pigou–Dalton principle of transfers. Finally, they show that the Method of Equal Shares provides $O(\log(k))$-multiplicative-1-additive-satisfaction approximation to the core.

4.4.3 Relaxation By Constraining the Space of Deviations

Yet another approach to relaxing the core property is to prohibit only certain types of deviations. As we have already explained at the beginning of this section, EJR can be viewed as a restricted variant of the core property: It prohibits the deviations of groups of voters towards outcomes T on which the deviating voters unanimously agree. Intuitively, if a group V agrees on all candidates from T, then it is easier for such a group to synchronise and to deviate, thus EJR can be viewed as the minimal restricted variant of the core. Motivated by the same arguments, Peters and Skowron [56] considered other restricted variants of the core property.

A *committee property* is a set of triples (A', k', W'), where (A', k') is an election instance and W' is a size-k' committee. We write $A|_V$ for profile A restricted to voters in $V \subseteq N$.

Definition 4.12 (Peters and Skowron [56]) Let $\mathcal{P}$ be a committee property. Given an instance (A, k), we say that a pair (V, T), with $V \neq \emptyset$, $V \subseteq N$, $T \subseteq C$, is an *allowed deviation* from a committee W if (1) $\frac{|T|}{k} \leq \frac{|V|}{n}$, (2) $|A(i) \cap T| > |A(i) \cap W|$ for each $i \in V$, and (3) T has property $\mathcal{P}$, i.e., $(A|_V, |T|, T) \in \mathcal{P}$. An ABC rule $\mathcal{R}$ satisfies the *core subject to* $\mathcal{P}$ if for each instance (A, k) and each winning committee $W \in \mathcal{R}(A, k)$ there exists no allowed deviation.

For example, let $\mathcal{P}_{\text{coh}}$ be a committee property such that $(A', k', W') \in \mathcal{P}_{\text{coh}}$ if and only if $W' \subseteq A'(i)$ for all voters i in the domain of A'; we call $\mathcal{P}_{\text{coh}}$ cohesiveness (cf. Definition 4.2). Then, EJR can be equivalently defined as the core subject to cohesiveness.

The Method of Equal Shares satisfies core subject to priceability with equal payments, which is a variant of priceability that additionally requires that voters must pay the same amount of virtual budget for the same candidate (cf. Definition 4.8);

priceability with equal payments is thus stronger than priceability, yet weaker than cohesiveness [56]. It is an open question whether the core subject to weaker (yet still natural) types of constraints is always non-empty.

4.5 Degressive and Regressive Proportionality

The notions of proportionality that we discussed in Sects. 4.1–4.4 aimed at capturing the following intuitive idea: An α fraction of voters should be able to decide about an α fraction of the committee—in this approach the relation between the size of the group and its eligibility is linear. In this section we discuss two alternative concepts: degressive and regressive proportionality. These two concepts should be viewed more as high-level ideas than formal properties. We first explain them intuitively, providing an illustrative example, and next we will discuss a few formal approaches to reasoning about degressive and regressive proportionality.

According to *degressive* proportionality, smaller groups of voters should be favoured, i.e., be eligible to more representatives in the elected committee than in the case of linear proportionality.[11] An extreme form of degressive proportionality is *diversity* [32]—there, if possible, each voter should be represented by at least one candidate in the elected committee. At the other end is the idea of *regressive* proportionality, where the emphasis is put on well-representing large groups. An extreme form of regressive proportionality is *individual excellence* [32], where it is assumed that only the candidates with the highest total support from the voters should be elected. In fact, these two notions—diversity and individual excellence—are extreme to the extent that they can no longer be considered notions of proportionality. Example 4.9, below, illustrates the ideas of degressive and regressive proportionality, and the two extreme variants of them—diversity and individual excellence.

Example 4.9 Consider the approval-based preference profile from Example 4.1:

60 voters: $\{a_1, \ldots, a_{10}\}$ 20 voters: $\{b_1, \ldots, b_6\}$ 10 voters: $\{c_1, c_2\}$
8 voters: $\{d_1, \ldots, a_4\}$ 2 voters: $\{e_1, e_2, e_3\}$.

A linearly-proportional committee W_1 could consist of six candidates from A, two candidates from B, one candidate from C, and one candidate from D (this is the committee selected by the Sainte-Laguë apportionment method). Another linearly-proportional committee could consist of seven candidates candidates from A, two from B, one from C, but none from D (this is the committee selected by the D'Hondt apportionment method).

---

[11] Degressive proportional apportionment is often used for distributing parliamentary seats among geographical regions, e.g., in the division of the European Parliament seats among EU countries (see the book of Rose [64] for a discussion of arguments and negotiations that resulted in a degressive apportionment rule being used for assembling the European Parliament).

Table 4.2 Flavors of (dis)proportionality

# Votes	60	20	10	8	2
Example of linear proportionality (Sainte-Laguë)	6	2	1	1	0
A different example of linear proportionality (D'Hondt)	7	2	1	0	0
An example of degressive proportionality	4	3	2	1	0
Another example of degressive proportionality	3	3	3	1	0
An example of diversity	4	3	1	1	1
Another example of diversity	2	2	2	2	2
An example of regressive proportionality	8	2	0	0	0
Individual excellence	10	0	0	0	0

In contrast, a degressive-proportional committee W_2 could, for example, consist of four candidates from A, three candidates from B, two candidates from C, and one candidate from D. Another example of a degressive-proportional committee would be W_3 with three candidates from each of the sets A, B, and C, and one from D. Committees W_2 and W_3, however, are not diverse, since two voters who support $E = \{e_1, e_2, e_3\}$ are not represented at all. A diverse committee could consist of, e.g., four candidates from A, three candidates from B, one candidates from C, one candidate from D, and one candidate from E. A regressive-proportional committee would include more candidates from the set $A = \{a_1, \ldots, a_{10}\}$ at the cost of groups supported by less voters. For example, a committee that consists of eight candidates from A and two candidates from B would be regressive-proportional. Table 4.2 shows the example relations between a size of a group and its number of representatives for different forms of proportionality:

The arguments in favour of degressive proportionality usually come from the analysis of probabilistic models describing how the decisions made by the elected committee map to the satisfaction of individual voters participating in the process of electing the committee (for party-list preferences, an excellent exposition is given by Koriyama et al. [41]; see also [47, 48]). An interesting concrete example of degressive proportionality is square-root proportionality devised by Penrose [53] (see also [70]), where the idea is that the groups of voters should be represented proportionally to the square-roots of their sizes.[12] Further, degressive proportionally in general, and diversity in particular, are particularly appealing ideas in the context of deliberative democracy—there, the goal is to select a committee that should discuss and deliberate on various issues rather than make majoritarian decisions. It is argued that for deliberative democracy it is particularly important to represent as many

---

[12] This method has been proposed for the United Nations Parliamentary Assembly [17] and for allocating voting weights in the Council of the European Union [71].

various opinions in the committees as possible [21, 50], which can be achieved by maximising the number of voters who are represented in the elected committee.

On the other hand, the idea of regressive proportionality is particularly appealing when the goal is to select a committee of candidates based on their individual merits, for example when the goal of an election is to select finalists in a contest or to choose a set of grants that should be funded (then, the voters act as judges/experts).

In the remaining part of this section we discuss two approaches to formalising the ideas of degressive and regressive proportionality: axiomatic approaches and a quantitative approach.

4.5.1 Axiomatic Approaches to Diversity and Individual Excellence

The axiomatic approach generally applies only to the extreme forms of the degressive and regressive proportionality, i.e., to diversity and individual excellence, respectively. This approach is similar to the one we discussed in Sect. 4.1: by formalising the concepts of diversity and individual excellence on party-list profiles (Definition 4.1), we obtain axiomatic characterisations for the more general domain of ABC rules.

Intuitively, disjoint diversity requires that in party-list profiles as many voters as possible have at least one representative in the elected committee. Disjoint equality says that each approval carries the same strength, and so all candidates that are approved once have the same right for being elected.

Definition 4.13 (*Disjoint diversity*) An ABC rule $\mathcal{R}$ satisfies *disjoint diversity* if for each party-list instance (A, k) with voter sets $(N_1, \ldots, N_p)$ and $|N_1| \geq |N_2| \geq \ldots \geq |N_p|$, there exists a winning committee $W \in \mathcal{R}(A, k)$ that contains one candidate for each of the k largest parties, i.e., for each $r \leq \min(p, k)$ and each $i \in N_r$ we have that $A(i) \cap W \neq \emptyset$.

Definition 4.14 (*Disjoint equality*) An ABC rule $\mathcal{R}$ satisfies *disjoint equality* if for each election instance (A, k) where each candidate is approved at most once and the number of approved candidates is at least k (i.e., $|\bigcup_{i \in N} A(i)| \geq k$), a committee W is winning if and only if it contains only approved candidates, $W \subseteq \bigcup_{i \in N} A(i)$.

Intuitively, disjoint equality is aimed at capturing the idea of individual excellence—the candidates that are approved exactly once are virtually indistinguishable from the perspective of the support coming from the voters; thus all such candidates should have equal rights to be selected.

The following theorems show that, similarly to the case of D'Hondt proportionality (Theorem 4.2), the concepts of disjoint diversity and disjoint equality uniquely extend to the full domain of approval-based preferences if one assumes the natural axioms of anonymity, neutrality, and consistency (and a few more technical axioms).

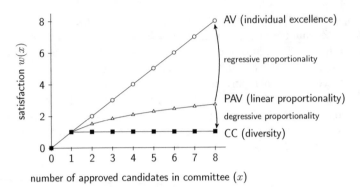

Fig. 4.2 A diagram illustrating the relation between defining w-functions of Thiele methods and the type of proportionality these Thiele rules implement

Theorem 4.6 (Lackner and Skowron [44]) *The Approval Chamberlin–Courant rule is the only non-trivial ABC ranking rule that satisfies anonymity, neutrality, consistency, weak efficiency, continuity, and disjoint diversity. Multi-Winner Approval Voting is the only ABC ranking rule that satisfies anonymity, neutrality, consistency, weak efficiency, continuity, and disjoint equality.*

Lackner and Skowron [44] provided a similar analysis for intermediate notions of degressive and regressive proportionality. They conclude that w-Thiele methods based on w-scoring functions that have a larger slope than the w-function of PAV are more oriented towards regressive proportionality, whereas w-functions that have a smaller slope are closer in spirit to the idea of degressive proportionality. This relation is symbolically visualised in Fig. 4.2.

Jaworski and Skowron [37] constructed a class of rules that generalise Phragmén's rule. Intuitively, a degressive variant of seq-Phragmén is obtained by assuming that the voters who already have more representatives earn money at a slower rate than those that have fewer. Regressive proportionality is implemented by assuming that the candidates who are approved by more voters cost less than those that garnered fewer approvals.

Faliszewski et al. [33] discuss three specific classes of rules that span the spectrum between individual excellence and diversity. They analyse these rules in the ranking-based model, that is when voters rank the candidates instead of approving some of them (see Sect. 6.1). These classes of rules can be analogously defined for approval ballots. Brill et al. [14], Faliszewski and Talmon [31] extend Monroe's rule so that it can implement the idea of regressive proportionality; this is also done in the ranking-based framework. It would be interesting to see whether their techniques can be successfully applied to the ABC model.

Finally, Subiza and Peris [72] propose an axiom called α-unanimity (parameterized with $\alpha \in [0, 1]$), which can be seen as a strong diversity axiom. The authors propose a voting rule (Lexiunanimous Approval Voting) that satisfies this axiom; this rule is a refined version of CC. Thiele methods (including CC itself) do not satisfy this axiom for any α.

4.5.2 Quantifying Degressive and Regressive Proportionality

The second approach to formally reason about degressive and regressive proportionality is quantitative in nature. Lackner and Skowron [43] define two measures—the utilitarian guarantee and the representation guarantee—that can be used to quantify how well a given rule performs in terms of individual excellence and diversity.

Recall that $\text{score}_{\text{AV}}(A, W)$ denotes the total number of approvals a given committee receives in profile A and $\text{score}_{\text{CC}}(A, W)$ denotes the number of voters who approve at least one member of W.

Definition 4.15 (*Utilitarian and Representation Guarantee* [43]) The utilitarian guarantee of an ABC rule $\mathcal{R}$ is a function $\kappa_{\text{AV}} \colon \mathbb{N} \to [0, 1]$ that takes as input an integer k, representing the committee size, and is defined as:

$$\kappa_{\text{AV}}(k) = \inf_A \frac{\min_{W \in \mathcal{R}(A,k)} (\text{score}_{\text{AV}}(A, W))}{\max_{W \colon |W|=k} (\text{score}_{\text{AV}}(A, W))}.$$

The representation guarantee of an ABC rule $\mathcal{R}$ is a function $\kappa_{\text{CC}} \colon \mathbb{N} \to [0, 1]$ defined as:

$$\kappa_{\text{CC}}(k) = \inf_A \frac{\min_{W \in \mathcal{R}(A,k)} (\text{score}_{\text{CC}}(A, W))}{\max_{W \colon |W|=k} (\text{score}_{\text{CC}}(A, W))}.$$

Note that the utilitarian and the representation guarantee of an ABC rule $\mathcal{R}$ measure how well rule $\mathcal{R}$ approximates Multi-Winner Approval Voting and the Approval Chamberlin–Courant rule, respectively. These two rules embody the principles of diversity and individual excellence (cf. Theorem 4.6).

Lackner and Skowron [43] show that the utilitarian guarantee of PAV, sequential PAV, and seq-Phragmén is $\Theta(1/\sqrt{k})$; their representation guarantee is $1/2 + \Theta(1/k)$. CC and seq-CC achieve a better representation guarantee (of 1 and $1 - 1/e$, respectively), but their utilitarian guarantee is only $\Theta(1/k)$. In that sense, these three proportional rules (PAV, sequential PAV, and seq-Phragmén) can be viewed as a desirable compromise between the two guarantees. On the other, the authors also show that proportional rules are never an *optimal* compromise. Finally, p-geometric rules—the Thiele rules defined by $w_{p\text{-geom}}(x) = \sum_{i=1}^{x} (1/p)^i$—for different values of the parameter p span the whole spectrum from AV to CC. By adjusting the parameter p, one can obtain any desired compromise between the utilitarian and representation goals.

Elkind et al. [29] extend this work by considering the "price" of justified representation axioms: what are the optimal utilitarian and representation guarantees when requiring justified representation (Definition 4.6) or extended justified representation (Definition 4.3)? Their results show that already justified representation implies a utilitarian guarantee of no better than $2/\sqrt{k}$; the same holds for EJR. The consequences for the representation guarantee are less pronounced: JR does not restrict the representation guarantee (e.g., CC satisfies JR and has a representation guarantee of 1) and EJR is compatible with a representation guarantee of $\frac{3}{4}$.

4.5.3 An Experimental View on Degressive and Regressive Proportionality

Godziszewski et al. [35] visualised the structure of the committees produced by various ABC rules on histograms. They performed computer simulations in which the candidates and the voters were represented as points in the two-dimensional Euclidean space. Intuitively, a point corresponding to a voter or a candidate might represent their position in the spectrum of possible opinions regarding various issues. In each simulation the candidates and the voters were drawn from a given distribution, and a preference profile was constructed from the positions of the voters and the candidates. The main idea was that the voters are more likely to approve candidates whose corresponding points are closer to them, since their opinions resemble views of such candidates. Given a preference profile, a specific ABC rule was used to find a winning committee, and the points corresponding to the selected candidates were marked with red dots on the histogram of the respective rule. The experiment was repeated multiple times, and each time the dots were put on the same histogram. Thus, the density of red dots in a given area represent the probabilities that the candidates from this area are chosen for the winning committee. This idea was first proposed by Elkind et al. [28] in the context of ranking-based elections.

Such histograms give valuable insights into the nature of voting rules. We depict several of them in Fig. 4.3. In the left column of the figure, we depict distributions of the points representing the voters and the candidates: red areas correspond to the candidates, green areas to the voters, and olive areas correspond to both. The subsequent columns depict distributions of the elected candidates for six ABC rules. These histograms already illustrate the very different natures of the considered rules. For example, the distributions obtained for PAV and the sequential Phragmén's rule closely resemble distributions of the voters (which is exactly what one would expect from proportional rules), CC puts more emphasis on representing as diverse a spectrum of voters as possible, AV selects candidates that are in the centres of the distributions—the choice that corresponds to individual excellence. The Method of Equal Shares induces histograms that are in some sense between PAV and AV. Finally, the behaviour of Minimax AV (MAV) is inconsistent with our intuitive interpretation of proportionality in the Euclidean model.

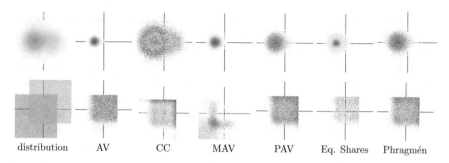

distribution   AV   CC   MAV   PAV   Eq. Shares   Phragmén

Fig. 4.3 Visualising the outcomes of some selected ABC rules (from [35])

The conclusions from this experimental exercise are to a large extent consistent with the conclusions coming from the axiomatic analysis. For a more detailed discussion we refer to the original work [35].

4.6 Proportionality and Strategic Voting

The ABC rules that we have considered in the context of proportionality are all prone to manipulations (cf. Sect. 3.6). In this section we explain that this is not a coincidence—achieving proportionality and strategyproofness at the same time is inherently impossible. This impossibility was first proven by Peters [54, 55] for resolute rules (rules that always return a single winning committee), even for very weak formulations of the desired axioms. (Earlier work by Aziz et al. [2] and Janson [36] already showed that certain proportional rules—such as PAV, seq-PAV, and seq-Phragmén—are not strategyproof.)

Theorem 4.7 (Peters [54, 55]) *Suppose $k \geq 3$, the number n of voters is divisible by k, and $m \geq k + 1$. Then there exists no resolute ABC rule $\mathcal{R}$ which satisfies the following three axioms:*

1. *weak proportionality: for each party-list election (A, k) where some singleton ballot $\{c\}$ appears at least n/k times $(|\{i : A(i) = \{c\}\}| \geq n/k)$, candidate c must belong to the winning committee, i.e., $c \in \mathcal{R}(A, k)$,*
2. *weak efficiency: a candidate who is approved by no voter may not be part of the winning committee, unless fewer than k candidates receive at least one approval,*
3. *inclusion-strategyproofness[13] (as defined in Sect. 3.6).*

Kluiving et al. [40] prove a similar result for irresolute rules (i.e., when rules are allowed to output multiple tied winning committees), using cardinality-strategyproofness and Pareto efficiency. Further, Duddy [27] proves a related impossibility

---

[13] This axiom can be further weakened to allow voters only to manipulate by reporting subsets of their true approval sets.

result for irresolute rules using slightly different axioms; this result also requires a form of Pareto efficiency.

Lackner and Skowron [42] showed that AV is the only ABC scoring rule (Sect. 3.5) that satisfies SD-strategyproofness; this result can also be seen as an impossibility result concerning proportionality and strategyproofness within the class of ABC scoring rules. Further, they quantified the trade-off between strategyproofness and proportionality. For various ABC rules they empirically measured their level of strategyproofness by assessing the fraction of profiles, for which there exists a voter who has an incentive to misreport her approval set. They concluded that rules which are more similar to AV (i.e., rules that follow the principle of regressive proportionality) are less manipulable than proportional rules. The rules that follow the principle of degressive proportionality are the most manipulable. A similar conclusion was obtained by Barrot et al. [6], but there the authors analysed a different class of rules—namely those based on the Hamming distance, and spanning the spectrum from AV to Minimax Approval Voting.

Since in the general case, there exist no proportional strategyproof ABC rule, Botan [9] restricted the analysis to three specific types of manipulations: (1) subset manipulations, where a voter can manipulate only by submitting a subset of her true approval set, (2) superset manipulations, where each voter can only send a superset of her true preferences, and (3) disjoint manipulations, where a manipulation can be performed only by submitting a subset of candidates disjoint from the true approval set of the voter. They showed that for party-list preference profiles (see Definition 4.1) all Thiele methods are cardinality-strategyproof[14] against subset, superset, and disjoint manipulations.

4.7 Proportionality with Respect to External Attributes

In Sects. 4.1–4.6, we have considered formal concepts that capture, in various ways, what it means that the structure of the elected committee proportionally reflects the (approval-based) preferences of the voters. In other words, we have considered proportionality with respect to the preferences given by the voters. In this section, we briefly consider a framework that approaches the concept of proportionality quite differently: we analyse proportionality with respect to external attributes of the candidates.[15]

Let us start by recalling the apportionment setting that we discussed in Sect. 4.1. In the apportionment model we are given a set of candidates, each candidate belonging to a single political party; for each political party we are given a desired fraction

---

[14] Formally, Botan [9] defines strategyproofness for irresolute rules and states their results for the general class of Gärdenfors preference extensions [34]. These extensions define preference relations over sets of winning committees and thus can be applied to irresolute rules.

[15] A noteworthy real-world example is the Lebanese Parliament, where an equal representation of Christians and Muslims (64 seats each) is mandated [26].

of seats the party should ideally get in the elected committee (typically, this is the fraction of votes cast on the party). The goal is to pick the committee that matches the desired fractions as closely as possible. Thus, one can say that in the apportionment setting there is one external attribute, which is the party affiliation, each candidate has a certain value of this attribute, and the goal is to pick the committee where the different values of the attribute are represented proportionally to the given desired fractions.

Now, assume that there are two attributes—each candidate has a political affiliation and a geographic region that she represents. For each value of each attribute we are given a desired fraction of seats that the candidates with this attribute value should get. This setting is called bi-apportionment, and it is discussed in detail in a book chapter by Pukelsheim [61] (several articles study the bi-apportionment setting from a computational perspective [46, 63, 67]). The model of bi-apportionment has been further extended to an arbitrary number of attributes by Lang and Skowron [45].[16] There, the authors analysed axiomatically and algorithmically two rules that extend the D'Hondt method and the largest remainder method to the multi-attribute apportionment.

The desired fractions in the (multi-attribute) apportionment model can be based on the voters preferences, or they might be given exogenously, e.g., by imposing certain quotas, specifying how many candidates with given attribute values should be included in the winning committee. Taking one specific interpretation, namely assuming the voters are asked to approve attribute values, Kagita et al. [39] proposed several other rules for selecting committees. They formulated axioms, requiring that the selected committee should consist of candidates whose attribute values proportionally represent voters' preferences. Unfortunately, none of the rules they propose satisfies any of these axioms. In general our axiomatic understanding of the multi-attribute apportionment model is still not well-advanced.

In the final part of this section we will consider a model which takes into account both the voters' preferences over candidates, and external constraints based on attributes of the candidates. Instead of defining this model formally, we provide an illustrative example.

Example 4.10 Assume we want to select a representative committee. Such a committee should be gender-balanced, containing 50% of male (M) and 50% of female (F) committee members. Additionally, the committee should represent people from different educational backgrounds: at least 25% and at most 50% of its members should have a bachelor's degree (B), between 40% and 60% should have an upper-secondary education (U), and between 10% and 25%—a primary or lower-secondary education (P). Finally, the selected committee should contain at least 25% young people (Y)

---

[16] The multi-attribute model finds its application, e.g., in the process of sortition. In sortition one needs to select a committee of ordinary people who will discuss certain controversial matters, and come up with recommendations helping the governments make decisions. In this process it is important to select a committee consisting of people who are representative for the whole society. Currently, randomised algorithms are mostly used for such selections [8]. The multi-attribute model provides alternative methods that take advantage of information regarding attributes of the potential committee members.

and at least 50% senior people (S). The pool of candidates from which we can select members of such a committee is given in the table below. Additionally, seven voters express their preferences via the following approval ballots.

Name	Gender	Education	Age
c_1	F	B	Y
c_2	M	U	Y
c_3	M	U	S
c_4	F	P	S
c_5	M	U	Y
c_6	M	U	Y
c_7	M	U	Y
c_8	F	B	S

$$A(1) = \{c_1, c_2, c_3\}$$
$$A(2) = \{c_3, c_5\}$$
$$A(3) = \{c_7, c_8\}$$
$$A(4) = \{c_3, c_4, c_5, c_7\}$$
$$A(5) = \{c_1, c_8\}$$
$$A(6) = \{c_6\}$$
$$A(7) = \{c_1, c_2, c_6\}$$

Assume we want to select $k = 4$ committee members. The winning committee according to AV would be $W_1 = \{c_1, c_3, c_7, c_8\}$ (for simplicity, we assume the ties are broken lexicographically $c_8 \succ c_7 \succ \cdots \succ c_1$), and according to PAV, the winning committee would be $W_2 = \{c_1, c_3, c_6, c_8\}$. However, each of these two committees violates the attribute-level constraints. The committee maximising the AV-score and the PAV-score subject to these constraints would be, respectively, $W_3 = \{c_1, c_3, c_4, c_7\}$ and $W_4 = \{c_3, c_4, c_6, c_8\}$.

As can be seen in Example 4.10, score-based ABC rules (in particular Thiele methods) are suitable for this approach: the winning committee is the one with the highest score that satisfies all external constraints. Following this approach, Bredereck et al. [10] and Celis et al. [18] considered the model of multi-winner elections with external constraints, but where the qualities of the committees are assessed via a general set function f. The function f may in particular depend on the voters' ballots, for example we can set $f(W) = \text{score}_{\text{AV}}(A, W)$. Aziz [1] studied a similar model, but assuming there is a global ranking over C that represents the objective qualities of the candidates. There, the goal is to select the lexicographically best committee subject to the multi-attribute constraints, which are treated more softly than in case of Bredereck et al. [10] and Celis et al. [18]. Let us also mention that Bei et al. [7] studied a related model, but there the goal is to select the committee of maximal cardinality that satisfies the attribute-level constraints. We will consider algorithmic aspects of these and related approaches in Sect. 5.3.

Note that this approach is not compatible with rules that do not naturally provide a ranking of committees by scores (e.g., seq-Phragmén or the Method of Equal Shares). It is an interesting question how to adapt these rules to the model with external constraints.

References

1. H. Aziz. A rule for committee selection with soft diversity constraints. *Group Decision and Negotiation*, 28:1193—1200, 2019.
2. H. Aziz, S. Gaspers, J. Gudmundsson, S. Mackenzie, N. Mattei, and T. Walsh. Computational aspects of multi-winner approval voting. In *Proceedings of the 14th International Conference on Autonomous Agents and Multiagent Systems (AAMAS-2015)*, pages 107–115, 2015.
3. H. Aziz, M. Brill, V. Conitzer, E. Elkind, R. Freeman, and T. Walsh. Justified representation in approval-based committee voting. *Social Choice and Welfare*, 48(2):461–485, 2017.
4. H. Aziz, E. Elkind, S. Huang, M. Lackner, L. Sánchez-Fernández, and P. Skowron. On the complexity of extended and proportional justified representation. In *Proceedings of the 32nd Conference on Artificial Intelligence (AAAI-2018)*, pages 902–909, 2018.
5. M. Balinski and H. P. Young. *Fair Representation: Meeting the Ideal of One Man, One Vote*. Yale University Press, 1982. (2nd Edition by Brookings Institution Press, 2001).
6. N. Barrot, J. Lang, and M. Yokoo. Manipulation of Hamming-based approval voting for multiple referenda and committee elections. In *Proceedings of the 16th International Conference on Autonomous Agents and Multiagent Systems (AAMAS-2017)*, pages 597–605, 2017.
7. X. Bei, S. Liu, C. K. Poon, and H. Wang. Candidate selections with proportional fairness constraints. In *Proceedings of the 19th International Conference on Autonomous Agents and Multiagent Systems (AAMAS-2020)*, pages 150–158, 2020.
8. G. Benadè, P. Gölz, and A. Procaccia. No stratification without representation. In *Proceedings of the 2019 ACM Conference on Economics and Computation (ACM-EC-2019)*, pages 281–314, 2019.
9. S. Botan. Manipulability of Thiele methods on party-list profiles. In *Proceedings of the 20th International Conference on Autonomous Agents and Multiagent Systems (AAMAS-2021)*, pages 223–231, 2021.
10. R. Bredereck, P. Faliszewski, A. Igarashi, M. Lackner, and P. Skowron. Multiwinner elections with diversity constraints. In *Proceedings of the 32nd Conference on Artificial Intelligence (AAAI-2018)*, pages 933–940, 2018.
11. R. Bredereck, P. Faliszewski, A. Kaczmarczyk, and R. Niedermeier. An experimental view on committees providing justified representation. In *Proceedings of the 28th International Joint Conference on Artificial Intelligence (IJCAI-2019)*, pages 109–115, 2019.
12. M. Brill, R. Freeman, S. Janson, and M. Lackner. Phragmén's voting methods and justified representation. In *Proceedings of the 31st Conference on Artificial Intelligence (AAAI-2017)*, pages 406–413, 2017. Extended version at https://arxiv.org/abs/2102.12305.
13. M. Brill, J.-F. Laslier, and P. Skowron. Multiwinner approval rules as apportionment methods. *Journal of Theoretical Politics*, 30(3):358–382, 2018.
14. M. Brill, P. Faliszewski, F. Sommer, and N. Talmon. Approximation algorithms for BalancedCC multiwinner rules. In *Proceedings of the 18th International Conference on Autonomous Agents and Multiagent Systems (AAMAS-2019)*, pages 494–502, 2019.
15. M. Brill, P. Gölz, D. Peters, U. Schmidt-Kraepelin, and K. Wilker. Approval-based apportionment. In *Proceedings of the 34th Conference on Artificial Intelligence (AAAI-2020)*, pages 1854–1861, 2020. Extended version at http://arxiv.org/abs/1911.08365.
16. M. Brill, J. Israel, E. Micha, and J. Peters. Individual representation in approval-based committee voting. In *Proceedings of the 36th Conference on Artificial Intelligence (AAAI-2022)*, pages 4892–4899, 2022.
17. A. Bummel. *The Composition of a Parliamentary Assembly at the United Nations*. Committee for a Democratic U.N., 2010.
18. L. E. Celis, L. Huang, and N. K. Vishnoi. Multiwinner voting with fairness constraints. In *Proceedings of the 27th International Joint Conference on Artificial Intelligence (IJCAI-2018)*, pages 144–151, 2018.
19. A. Cevallos and A. Stewart. A verifiably secure and proportional committee election rule. In *Proceedings of the 3rd ACM Conference on Advances in Financial Technologies*, pages 29–42, 2021.

20. G. Chalkiadakis, E. Elkind, and M. Wooldridge. Computational aspects of cooperative game theory. *Synthesis Lectures on Artificial Intelligence and Machine Learning*, 5(6):1–168, 2011.

21. B. Chamberlin and P. Courant. Representative deliberations and representative decisions: Proportional representation and the Borda rule. *American Political Science Review*, 77(3):718–733, 1983.

22. X. Chen, B. Fain, L. Lyu, and K. Munagala. Proportionally fair clustering. In *Proceedings of the 36th International Conference on Machine Learning (ICML-2019)*, volume 97, pages 1032–1041, 2019.

23. Y. Cheng, Z. Jiang, K. Munagala, and K. Wang. Group fairness in committee selection. In *Proceedings of the 2019 ACM Conference on Economics and Computation (ACM-EC-2019)*, pages 263–279. ACM, 2019.

24. V. D'Hondt. *Question électorale. La représentation proportionnelle des partis*. Bruylant, Bruxelles, 1878.

25. V. D'Hondt. *Exposé du système pratique de représentation proportionnelle adopté par le Comité de l'Associaton Réformiste Belge*. Van der Haegen, Ghent, 1885.

26. M. Diss and F. Steffen. The Distribution of Power in the Lebanese Parliament Revisited. Technical report, HAL, 2017. Working Paper.

27. C. Duddy. Electing a representative committee by approval ballot: An impossibility result. *Economics Letters*, 124(1):14–16, 2014.

28. E. Elkind, P. Faliszewski, J. Laslier, P. Skowron, A. Slinko, and N. Talmon. What do multiwinner voting rules do? An experiment over the two-dimensional euclidean domain. In *Proceedings of the 31st Conference on Artificial Intelligence (AAAI-2017)*, pages 494–501, 2017.

29. E. Elkind, P. Faliszewski, A. Igarashi, P. Manurangsi, U. Schmidt-Kraepelin, and W. Suksompong. The price of justified representation. *CoRR*, abs/2112.05994, 2021. URL https://arxiv.org/abs/2112.05994.

30. B. Fain, K. Munagala, and N. Shah. Fair allocation of indivisible public goods. In *Proceedings of the 2018 ACM Conference on Economics and Computation (ACM-EC-2018)*, pages 575–592. ACM, 2018. Extended version at http://arxiv.org/abs/1805.03164.

31. P. Faliszewski and N. Talmon. Between proportionality and diversity: Balancing district sizes under the Chamberlin-Courant rule. In *Proceedings of the 17th International Conference on Autonomous Agents and Multiagent Systems (AAMAS-2018)*, pages 14–22, 2018.

32. P. Faliszewski, P. Skowron, A. Slinko, and N. Talmon. Multiwinner voting: A new challenge for social choice theory. In U. Endriss, editor, *Trends in Computational Social Choice*, chapter 2, pages 27–47. AI Access, 2017.

33. P. Faliszewski, P. Skowron, A. Slinko, and N. Talmon. Multiwinner rules on paths from k-Borda to Chamberlin-Courant. In *Proceedings of the 26th International Joint Conference on Artificial Intelligence (IJCAI-2017)*, pages 192–198. ijcai.org, 2017.

34. P. Gärdenfors. On definitions of manipulation of social choice functions. In J.-J. Laffont, editor, *Aggregation and Revelation of Preferences*. North-Holland, 1979.

35. M. Godziszewski, P. Batko, P. Skowron, and P. Faliszewski. An analysis of approval-based committee rules for 2D-Euclidean elections. In *Proceedings of the 35th Conference on Artificial Intelligence (AAAI-2021)*, pages 5448–5455, 2021.

36. S. Janson. Phragmén's and Thiele's election methods. *CoRR*, abs/1611.08826, 2016. URL http://arxiv.org/abs/1611.08826.

37. M. Jaworski and P. Skowron. Phragmén rules for degressive and regressive proportionality. In *Proceedings of the 31st International Joint Conference on Artificial Intelligence (IJCAI-2022)*, pages 328–334, 2022.

38. Z. Jiang, K. Munagala, and K. Wang. Approximately stable committee selection. In *Proceedings of the 52nd Symposium on Theory of Computing (STOC-2020)*, pages 463–472. ACM, 2020.

39. V. R. Kagita, A. K. Pujari, V. Padmanabhan, H. Aziz, and V. Kumar. Committee selection using attribute approvals. In *Proceedings of the 20th International Conference on Autonomous Agents and Multiagent Systems (AAMAS-2021)*, pages 683–691, 2021.

40. B. Kluiving, A. Vries, P. Vrijbergen, A. Boixel, and U. Endriss. Analysing irresolute multiwinner voting rules with approval ballots via SAT solving. In *Proceedings of the 24th European*

Conference on Artificial Intelligence (ECAI-2020), volume 325 of Frontiers in Artificial Intelligence and Applications, pages 131–138. IOS Press, 2020.

41. Y. Koriyama, J.-F. Laslier, A. Macé, and R. Treibich. Optimal Apportionment. Journal of Political Economy, 121(3):584–608, 2013.

42. M. Lackner and P. Skowron. Approval-based multi-winner rules and strategic voting. In Proceedings of the 27th International Joint Conference on Artificial Intelligence (IJCAI-2018), pages 340–436, 2018.

43. M. Lackner and P. Skowron. Utilitarian welfare and representation guarantees of approval-based multiwinner rules. Artificial Intelligence, 288:103366, 2020.

44. M. Lackner and P. Skowron. Consistent approval-based multi-winner rules. Journal of Economic Theory, 192:105173, 2021.

45. J. Lang and P. Skowron. Multi-attribute proportional representation. Artificial Intelligence, 263:74–106, 2018.

46. I. Lari, F. Ricca, and A. Scozzari. Bidimensional allocation of seats via zero-one matrices with given line sums. Annals OR, 215(1):165–181, 2014.

47. J.-F. Laslier. Why not proportional? Mathematical Social Sciences, 63(2):90–93, 2012.

48. A. Macé and R. Treibich. Computing the optimal weights in a utilitarian model of apportionment. Mathematical Social Sciences, 63(2):141–151, 2012.

49. E. Micha and N. Shah. Proportionally fair clustering revisited. In Proceedings of the 47th International Colloquium on Automata, Languages, and Programming (ICALP-2020), pages 85:1–85:16, 2020.

50. B. Monroe. Fully proportional representation. American Political Science Review, 89(4):925–940, 1995.

51. K. Munagala, Y. Shen, K. Wang, and Z. Wang. Approximate core for committee selection via multilinear extension and market clearing. In Proceedings of the 33rd ACM-SIAM Symposium on Discrete Algorithms (SODA-2022), pages 2229–2252, 2022.

52. J. M. Osborne and A. Rubinstein. A Course in Game Theory, volume 1 of MIT Press Books. The MIT Press, 1994.

53. L. S. Penrose. The elementary statistics of majority voting. Journal of the Royal Statistical Society, 109(1):53–57, 1946.

54. D. Peters. Proportionality and strategyproofness in multiwinner elections. In Proceedings of the 17th International Conference on Autonomous Agents and Multiagent Systems (AAMAS-2018), pages 1549–1557, 2018.

55. D. Peters. Fair Division of the Commons. PhD thesis, University of Oxford, 9 2019.

56. D. Peters and P. Skowron. Proportionality and the limits of welfarism. In Proceedings of the 2020 ACM Conference on Economics and Computation (ACM-EC-2020), pages 793–794, 2020. Extended version at https://arxiv.org/abs/1911.11747.

57. D. Peters, G. Pierczynski, and P. Skowron. Proportional participatory budgeting with additive utilities. In Proceedings of the Thirty-fifth Conference on Neural Information Processing Systems (NeurIPS-2021), pages 12726–12737, 2021.

58. D. Peters, G. Pierczyski, N. Shah, and P. Skowron. Market-based explanations of collective decisions. In Proceedings of the 35th Conference on Artificial Intelligence (AAAI-2021), pages 5656–5663, 2021.

59. E. Phragmén. Proportionella val. En valteknisk studie. Svenska spörsmål 25. Lars Hökersbergs förlag, Stockholm, 1895.

60. G. Pierczynski and P. Skowron. Core-stable committees under restricted domains. CoRR, abs/2108.01987, 2021. URL https://arxiv.org/abs/2108.01987.

61. F. Pukelsheim. Proportional Representation: Apportionment Methods and Their Applications, chapter Representing Districts and Parties: Double Proportionality. Springer, 2014.

62. F. Pukelsheim. Proportional Representation: Apportionment Methods and Their Applications. Springer International Publishing, 2nd edition, 2017.

63. F. Pukelsheim, F. Ricca, B. Simeone, A. Scozzari, and P. Serafini. Network flow methods for electoral systems. Networks, 59(1):73–88, 2012.

64. R. Rose. *Representing Europeans: a pragmatic approach*. Oxford University Press, Oxford, 2013.
65. A. Sainte-Laguë. La représentation proportionnelle et la méthode des moindres carrés. In *Annales scientifiques de l'école Normale Supérieure*, volume 27, pages 529–542, 1910.
66. L. Sánchez-Fernández, E. Elkind, M. Lackner, N. Fernández, J. A. Fisteus, P. Basanta Val, and P. Skowron. Proportional justified representation. In *Proceedings of the 31st Conference on Artificial Intelligence (AAAI-2017)*, pages 670–676, 2017.
67. P. Serafini and B. Simeone. Parametric maximum flow methods for minimax approximation of target quotas in biproportional apportionment. *Networks*, 59(2):191–208, 2012.
68. P. Skowron. Proportionality degree of multiwinner rules. In *Proceedings of the 2021 ACM Conference on Economics and Computation (ACM-EC-2021)*, pages 820–840, 2021. Extended version at https://arxiv.org/abs/1810.08799.
69. P. Skowron, M. Lackner, M. Brill, D. Peters, and E. Elkind. Proportional rankings. In *Proceedings of the 26th International Joint Conference on Artificial Intelligence (IJCAI-2017)*, pages 409–415, 2017.
70. W. Słomczyński and K. Życzkowski. Penrose voting system and optimal quota. *Acta Physica Polonica*, B 37:3133–3143, 2006.
71. W. Słomczyński and K. Życzkowski. Degressive proportionality in the european union. In *The Composition of the European Parliament. Workshop 30 January 2017*, pages 37–48, 2017.
72. B. Subiza and J. E. Peris. A representative committee by approval balloting. *Group Decision and Negotiation*, 26(5):1029–1040, 2017.
73. T. N. Thiele. Om flerfoldsvalg. In *Oversigt over det Kongelige Danske Videnskabernes Selskabs Forhandlinger*, pages 415–441. 1895.

Chapter 5
Algorithms and Computational Complexity

In this chapter, we discuss computational problems related to ABC rules and algorithms that solve these problems. We start by discussing the computational complexity of ABC rules. As many ABC rules are computationally difficult, a thorough algorithmic analysis is paramount to a practical application of these rules. We consider algorithmic techniques such as integer linear programming, fixed-parameter algorithms, approximation algorithms, and algorithms for structured domains. Moreover, we discuss computational questions related to proportionality and to strategic voting.

5.1 Computational Complexity

How computationally expensive is it to find a winning committee according to a given ABC rule? Clearly, this question is of major importance for the practical use of an ABC rule. Here, we distinguish only two types of complexity: ABC rules that are computationally easy, i.e., computable in polynomial time, and ABC rules that are computationally expensive, i.e., those that are NP-hard. Note that this is only a coarse dichotomy; we discuss its implications further below.

Let us first consider the class of Thiele methods. Out of the three most prominent Thiele methods, two are NP-hard (CC and PAV) and one is computable in polynomial time (AV). A polynomial-time algorithm for AV is straightforward: for each alternative c we compute its approval score $\text{score}_{AV}(A, c) = |\{i \in N : c \in A(i)\}|$ and select the k alternatives with the largest scores. To be able to claim NP-hardness of an ABC rule $\mathcal{R}$, we have to fix a decision problem; we choose the following for rules based on scores: given an approval profile, is there a committee with $\mathcal{R}$-score at least s? The NP-hardness of CC has been shown by Procaccia et al. [55]; the NP-hardness of PAV by Skowron et al. [59] and Aziz et al. [1] (for different decision problems). A more general result shows that a large class of Thiele methods is NP-hard:

© The Author(s) 2023
M. Lackner and P. Skowron, *Multi-Winner Voting with Approval Preferences*,
SpringerBriefs in Intelligent Systems, https://doi.org/10.1007/978-3-031-09016-5_5

Theorem 5.1 ([59, Theorem 5]) *Let $w : \mathbb{N} \to \mathbb{R}$ be a non-decreasing function for which $w(i) - w(i-1) > w(i+1) - w(i)$ for some $i \in \mathbb{N}$. Given an approval profile profile A, a committee size k, and a bound s, it is NP-hard to decide whether there exists a committee of size k with a w-score of at least s, i.e., $\mathrm{score}_w(A, W) \geq s$.*

Note that this theorem does not apply to AV, which is indeed polynomial-time computable. Interestingly, a similar result also holds for 2D-Euclidean preferences. We say that an approval profile is 2D-Euclidean if the voters and the candidates can be represented in the two-dimensional Euclidean space so that for each voter i the following holds: if i approves a candidate c, then she also approves all candidates that are closer to i than c. The following theorem applies, e.g., to PAV and CC.

Theorem 5.2 (Godziszewski et al. [36]) *Let $w : \mathbb{N} \to \mathbb{R}$ be a non-linear and concave function. Given a 2D-Euclidean approval profile profile A, a committee size k, and a bound s, it is NP-hard to decide if there is a k-size committee with a w-score of at least s.*

Winning committees of sequential and reverse sequential Thiele methods can be computed in polynomial time; this follows immediately from their definitions. The same holds for Greedy Monroe, seq-Phragmén, the Method of Equal Shares, and SAV. In contrast, appropriate decision problems for Monroe's rule [55], lexical-Phragmén [15], and MAV [40] are NP-complete. The NP-hardness for MAV also holds for 2D-Euclidean preferences [36]. These complexity results are summarised in Table 3.1.

To conclude, the complexity classification discussed here should not be misunderstood in implying that NP-hard ABC rules are impractical and should be avoided. There is a wide range of algorithmic techniques available to solve NP-hard problems, and many disciplines in computer science encounter (and routinely solve) computationally hard problems. Instead the message here is the following: When using a polynomial-time computable rule, even very large instances can be expected to be solved quickly. For NP-hard rules, a more thorough analysis is necessary to determine how large instances can be solved (cf. Sect. 5.2).

5.2 How to Compute Winning Committees?

The arguably most central algorithmic question is: how to compute winning committees for an ABC voting rule? Clearly, the answer significantly differs from rule to rule. Rules that can be computed in polynomial time generally do not require sophisticated algorithms. In particular, algorithms for AV, SAV, as well as for sequential and reverse sequential Thiele methods follow immediately from their corresponding definitions. Algorithms for Phragmén's sequential rule and the Method of Equal Shares are slightly more involved but also do not require more than a careful adaption of the corresponding mathematical definitions. (Note that for seq-Phragmén it is more convenient to implement its discrete formulation.) For rules that are NP-hard to compute, we discuss four algorithmic methods in the following: integer linear programs, fixed-parameter algorithms, approximation algorithms, and algorithms for structured domains.

5.2.1 Integer Linear Programs (ILPs)

The most common approach to compute NP-hard ABC rules is to employ integer linear program (ILP) solvers, such as Gurobi or CPLEX. These are fast, general purpose solvers used for hard optimisation problems. To use such a solver, one has to encode an ABC rule as a integer linear program, i.e., a system of linear inequalities constraining a linear expression that is maximised or minimised. We will see two examples of ILPs in the following. Several ILPs (including these two) are available in the abcvoting Python library [38].

The ILP displayed in Fig. 5.1 shows how PAV can be expressed in such a form. This particular ILP formulation for PAV is taken from Peters and Lackner [51]. Two types of variables are used here: $x_{i,\ell}$ intuitively encodes that voter i approves at least ℓ candidates in the committee, and y_c encodes that candidate c is contained in the winning committee. Given an election instance (A, k), this ILP maximises the PAV-score expressed in (5.1). Further it ensures that exactly k candidates are selected with Eq. (5.4) and that $x_{i,\ell}$ indeed encodes that voter i approves at least ℓ candidates in the committee with Eq. (5.5). Note that it can occur that $x_{i,\ell} = 0$ and $x_{i,\ell+1} = 1$, but this is never an optimal solution since $\frac{1}{\ell} > \frac{1}{\ell+1}$. It is easy to see that this ILP can be adapted for computing other Thiele methods by adjusting the optimisation goal in (5.1). Another ILP formulation is due to Skowron et al. [59]. This ILP is applicable to a larger class of multi-winner rules (OWA rules).

As a second example of an ILP encoding, we present one for MAV in Fig. 5.2. Here, y_c encodes whether candidate c is contained in the winning committee, $d_{i,c}$ encodes whether voter i disagrees with the decision of whether c is in the committee

$$\text{maximise} \quad \sum_{i=1}^{n} \sum_{\ell=1}^{k} \frac{1}{\ell} \cdot x_{i,\ell} \tag{5.1}$$

$$\text{subject to:} \quad x_{i,\ell} \in \{0,1\} \qquad \text{for } i \in [n], \ell \in [k] \tag{5.2}$$

$$y_c \in \{0,1\} \qquad \text{for } c \in C \tag{5.3}$$

$$\sum_{c \in C} y_c = k \tag{5.4}$$

$$\sum_{\ell=1}^{k} x_{i,\ell} = \sum_{c \in A(i)} y_c \qquad \text{for } i \in [n] \tag{5.5}$$

Fig. 5.1 An ILP for computing PAV

$$
\begin{aligned}
&\text{minimise} \quad D \\
&\text{subject to:} \quad d_{i,c} \in \{0,1\} && \text{for } i \in [n], c \in C \\
&\qquad\qquad\quad y_c \in \{0,1\} && \text{for } c \in C \\
&\qquad\qquad\quad \sum_{c \in C} y_c = k \\
&\qquad\qquad\quad d_{i,c} = 1 - y_c && \text{for } c \in A(i) && (5.6) \\
&\qquad\qquad\quad d_{i,c} = y_c && \text{for } c \in C \setminus A(i) && (5.7) \\
&\qquad\qquad\quad \sum_{c \in C} d_{i,c} \leq D && && (5.8)
\end{aligned}
$$

Fig. 5.2 An ILP for computing MAV

or not, and D is the maximum Hamming distance between a voter and the chosen committee. Constraints (5.6) and (5.7) fix the value of $d_{i,c}$, i.e.,

$$
d_{i,c} = \begin{cases} 0 & \text{if } (c \in A(i) \text{ and } y_c = 1) \text{ or } (c \notin A(i) \text{ and } y_c = 0), \\ 1 & \text{otherwise.} \end{cases}
$$

Then, $\sum_{c \in C} d_{i,c}$ is the Hamming distance between the committee defined by y_c and $A(i)$. Due to Constraint (5.8), these sums are $\leq D$ for all voters. Hence, by minimising D, we minimise the maximum distance.

Lastly, for Monroe's rule, Pottho and Brams [54] discuss ILP formulations, and for lexical-Phragmén an ILP is due to Brill et al. [15].

5.2.2 Fixed-Parameter Algorithms

Fixed-parameter algorithms have received some attention for ABC rules. The main idea is to identify a parameter of the problem (ideally one that is small in practice) and search for algorithms that require only polynomial time when this parameter is constant. A fixed-parameter tractable (FPT) algorithm for a parameter p is one with a runtime of $O(f(p) \cdot \text{poly}(m, n))$, where f is an arbitrary, typically exponential function. Let us mention three natural parameters in the context of multi-winner elections: the number of candidates (m), the committee size k, and the number of voters n.

Let us first discuss the parameter m, i.e., the number of candidates. As there are $\binom{m}{k} \leq m^m$ committees, it is possible to consider each possible committee in an FPT algorithm. This bound gives trivial (and uninteresting) FPT results for most NP-hard rules. For example, for w-Thiele methods one can compute $\text{score}_w(A, W)$ for each committee W and pick those with maximum score. An interesting exception is Monroe, where it is not immediately obvious how to compute the Monroe score of a given committee in polynomial time. This is achievable via a reduction to the min-cost max-flow problem, described by Procaccia et al. [55].

For the parameter committee size k, most results are negative: First, Betzler et al. [9] show for Monroe and CC that it is W[2]-hard to verify whether a committee exists with at least a certain Monroe-/CC-score. These hardness results continue to hold even if the number of unrepresented voters is used as an additional parameter [9]. Second, Misra et al. [48] show an analogous W[2]-hardness result for MAV. Third, Aziz et al. [1] show for all Thiele methods with $2w(1) > w(2)$ that testing whether a committee is winning is coW[1]-hard.[1] All these results imply that one cannot hope for an FPT algorithm computing these ABC rules, i.e., it is unlikely that an algorithm exists with a runtime of, e.g., $O(2^k \cdot \text{poly}(m, n))$.

The parameter n, the number of voters, is a natural choice if multi-winner elections are conducted in small groups and leads to interesting algorithms. Betzler et al. [9] show that CC and Monroe can be solved in time $n^n \cdot \text{poly}(m, n)$. In a similar vein, Faliszewski et al. [32] show an FPT result with respect to n for a large class of multi-winner voting rules (including Thiele methods). Their algorithm is based on mixed integer linear programming and Lenstra's result [41] that (mixed) integer linear programs can be solved in FPT time with the number of variables as parameter.[2] The results from Faliszewski et al. [32] have been substantially generalised by Bredereck et al. [13], including an FPT result for Thiele methods with weighted voters.

Moreover, Betzler et al. [9] provide a thorough and detailed parameterized complexity analysis for CC and Monroe for further parameters (e.g., the number of unrepresented voters) but find mostly hardness results. Yang and Wang [64] give an overview of further parameterized results; however, the concrete results announced in this short paper are not published yet.

To conclude, let us report on a positive result for MAV: MAV can be computed in time $O(d^{2d})$, where d is the optimal MAV-score, as shown by Misra et al. [48].[3] This runtime is essentially optimal subject to a standard complexity theoretic assumption, as shown by Cygan et al. [22].

5.2.3 Approximation Algorithms

The most natural approximation algorithm for Thiele methods are their sequential variants, as described in Sect. 2.3. Sequential w-Thiele provides a very good approximation of w-Thiele [44, 59]; this follows directly from a more general approximation result for submodular set functions by Nemhauser et al. [49].

---

[1] The condition $2w(1) > w(2)$ excludes AV but is satisfied for PAV and CC.

[2] We refer the interested reader to Gavenčiak et al. [34] a general overview of how integer linear programming can be used to find FPT algorithms.

[3] Misra et al. [48] claimed that the runtime of their algorithm is d^d; this was corrected later [22, 43].

Table 5.1 Guarantees of the approximation algorithms for the most prominent Thiele methods. The approximation ratios of the algorithms of Lu and Boutilier [44] and Dudycz et al. [24] are tight unless P = NP. They are also tight for the algorithms that run in $f(k) \cdot n^{o(k)}$ time assuming the Gap Exponential Time Hypothesis (Gap-ETH). The approximation ratio of the algorithm of Barman et al. [4] is tight assuming Unique Games Conjecture

	w-function	Approximation ratio	References
CC	$w(x) = \min(x, 1)$	$1 - 1/e$	Lu and Boutilier [44]
ℓ-best	$w(x) = \min(x, \ell)$	$1 - \frac{\ell^\ell}{e^\ell \cdot \ell!}$	Barman et al. [4]
PAV	$w(x) = \sum_{i=1}^{x} \frac{1}{i}$	0.7965	Dudycz et al. [24]
SLAV	$w(x) = \sum_{i=1}^{x} \frac{1}{2i-1}$	0.7394	Dudycz et al. [24]
Penrose	$w(x) = \sum_{i=1}^{x} \frac{1}{i^2}$	0.7084	Dudycz et al. [24]

Theorem 5.3 (Lu and Boutilier [44] and Skowron et al. [59]) *Sequential w-Thiele is a 0.63-approximation algorithm for w-Thiele. More specifically, Sequential w-Thiele achieves a w-score of at least $1 - (1 - 1/k)^k \geq 1 - 1/e \geq 0.63$ times the optimal w-score.*

Dudycz et al. [24] designed an algorithm that gives stronger approximation guarantees than $(1 - 1/e)$ for w-Thiele methods for which the derivatives of the defining w-function decrease slower than a geometric sequence. The algorithm is based on pipage rounding of the fractional solution returned by a linear program. Barman et al. [4] provided a $\left(1 - \frac{\ell^\ell}{e^\ell \cdot \ell!}\right)$-approximation algorithm for the w-Thiele function with $w(x) = \min(x, \ell)$. Table 5.1 summaries the guarantees of the best approximation algorithms for most prominent Thiele methods. Notably, under standard assumptions, all these guarantees cannot be improved within the class of algorithms running in polynomial time.

One can also find approximation algorithms for the corresponding *minimisation* problem: for w-Thiele, instead of maximising the w-score, one can equivalently minimise the difference from the theoretical optimum of $n \cdot w(k)$, i.e., to minimise the w-loss defined as $\text{loss}_w(A, W) = n \cdot w(k) - \text{score}_w(A, W)$. The minimisation and the maximisation variants of the problem have the same optimal solutions, but they differ in terms of approximability. If the optimal committee W has a high score, i.e., if $\text{score}_w(A, W)$ is close to $n \cdot w(k)$, then an approximation algorithm for the minimisation variant would be superior. For instance, if for the optimal committee W we have $\text{score}_w(A, W) = 0.95 \cdot n \cdot w(k)$, then a 2-approximation algorithm for the minimisation variant of the problem is guaranteed to return a solution with the score at least as high as $0.9 \cdot n \cdot w(k)$. On the other hand, a $1/2$-approximation algorithm for the maximisation variant may return a committee with score equal to $0.475 \cdot n \cdot w(k)$. Conversely, if the the optimal committee has a significantly lower score than $n \cdot w(k)$, then a good approximation algorithm for the maximisation variant of the problem will produce better committees.

Byrka et al. [17] present a 2.36-approximation algorithm for PAV according to this loss_w measure. This algorithm is based on dependent rounding of a linear program solution. It is notable that this result does not hold for arbitrary weights; in particular, such an approximation algorithm does not exist for CC under the assumption that $P \neq NP$ [17]. While seq-PAV can be viewed as a voting rule in its own right, this is more debatable for such a rounding-based algorithm. In particular, it cannot be expected to satisfy nice axiomatic properties such as committee monotonicity, and thus constitutes first and foremost an approximation of PAV.

Skowron [57] describes two alternative algorithms that for certain Thiele methods (including PAV and CC) can provide arbitrarily good approximation guarantees and that work in FPT time for the parameter (k, t), where t is the upper-bound on the number of candidates each voter approves. Thus, these algorithms are practical only when the desired size of the committee k and the approval sets of the voters are all small. Moreover, Skowron [57] shows that if each voter approves sufficiently many candidates, then Sequential w-Thiele provides an even better approximation guarantee than 0.63. Analogous results, but with the focus on CC, are due to Skowron and Faliszewski [58].

For MAV, stronger approximation results hold: Byrka and Sornat [16] and Cygan et al. [22] present polynomial-time approximation schemes (PTAS) for MAV, i.e., polynomial-time approximation algorithms that achieves arbitrary (but fixed) precision; previous work established first a 3-approximation algorithm (LeGrand et al. [40]) and then a 2-approximation algorithm (Caragiannis et al. [18]).

5.2.4 Algorithms for Structured Domains

The fourth and final algorithmic technique is to consider structured preference domains. Here, the assumption is that preference profiles possess some combinatorial structure that gives algorithmic advantages. We refer the interested reader to a survey by Elkind et al. [27] that discusses this topic more broadly. For our purpose here, we would like to discuss only two restrictions: candidate and voter interval (defined by Elkind and Lackner [25], based on previous work by Dietrich and List [30], Faliszewski et al. [23], List [42]), but we note that many other restrictions exist and have been studied extensively [25, 26, 33, 50, 62, 63].

A profile A belongs to the candidate interval (CI) domain if there exists a linear order of candidates such that for each voter $i \in N$, the set $A(i)$ appears contiguously on the linear order. Similarly, a profile A belongs to the voter interval (VI) domain if there exists a linear order of voters such that for each voter $c \in C$, the set $N(c)$ appears contiguously on the linear order. The CI domain is closely related to the single-peaked domain for arbitrary ordinal preferences and the VI domain is similar to the single-crossing domain; this is analysed in more detail by Elkind and Lackner [25].

Under the assumption that preferences belong either to the CI or VI domain, the computational complexity can change dramatically: MAV is solvable in polynomial time if the given approval profile belongs either to the CI or VI domain [43]. Further, Thiele methods (Peters and Lackner [51]) and Monroe's rule (Betzler et al. [9]) can be solved in polynomial time if the given approval profile belongs to the CI domain. It remains an open problem whether the same holds for the VI domain.

5.3 The Algorithmic Perspective on Proportionality

In this section, we briefly review the literature that deals with the computational problem of finding a proportional committee.

5.3.1 Finding Proportional Committees for Cohesive Groups

We first look at the proportionality concepts that formalise the behaviour of rules with respect to cohesive groups of voters; see Sect. 4.2.

Note that even the problem of deciding whether in a given instance of election there exists an ℓ-cohesive group of voters is NP-complete [60]. Similarly, given a committee W, deciding whether W satisfies the EJR condition is coNP-complete [2]; the same holds for the problem of deciding whether W satisfies the PJR condition [3]. Checking if a given committee W satisfies JR is computationally easy—for each candidate one needs to check whether the group of voters approving this candidate is 1-cohesive, and if so, to check if less than n/k voters from such a group are left without a representative in W. Checking whether a given committee satisfies perfect representation (Definition 4.9) is also computationally easy—the problem reduces to finding a perfect constrained matching in a bipartite graph [56].

While the problem of checking if a given committee satisfies the EJR/PJR condition is computationally hard, for a given election instance one can find in polynomial time *some* committee that satisfies the two conditions (e.g., through the Method of Equal Shares [52], or through a local-search algorithm for PAV [3]). The situation is quite different for perfect representation (PR): it is NP-complete to check whether there exists a PR committee for a given election instance [56]. Consequently, unless $P = NP$, there exists no polynomial-time ABC rule that satisfies perfect representation.

5.3.2 Finding Committees with Attribute-Level Constraints

Next, we move to the model with external attribute-level constraints from Sect. 4.7.

We start by considering the model from Example 4.10, where we have a set of voters with approval-based preferences over the candidates, the candidates have attribute values (the attributes can be, e.g., gender, age group, education level, etc.) and for each attribute value we are given quotas specifying upper and lower limits on the number of committee members with this particular attribute value. Two recent works by Bredereck et al. [12] and Celis et al. [20] considered algorithmic aspects of the problem of finding committees maximising a certain score, subject to given attribute-level constraints. The authors considered the problem from the perspective of approximation algorithms and parameterized complexity theory, as well as variants of the problem where the attribute-level constraints have certain special structures. We do not describe their results in detail as the specific results are obtained for the ranking-based multi-winner model (see Sect. 6.1). However, it is worth mentioning that even the problem of finding a committee that satisfies the attribute-level constraints is computationally hard. Approximation and fixed-parameter tractable algorithms for this simpler problem were studied by Lang and Skowron [39].

A very similar model to the one from Example 4.10 is *constrained approval voting (CAP)* (Brams [10], Potthoff [53]). The main difference to the previously discussed model is that CAP uses constraints formulated for combinations of attributes. For example, a constraint can have the following form: "the proportion of young (Y) males (M) with higher education (H) in the committee should not exceed 14%". Specifically, Brams [10] and Potthoff [53] suggest to pick the committee that maximises the AV score subject to the aforementioned combinatorial constraints. A direct translation of CAP into an ILP problem was given by Straszak et al. [61]. In general, the setting of constrained approval voting has not been thoroughly studied in its full generality, and the model is fairly unexplored from a computational perspective.

Finally, the computational problem of finding a committee subject to attribute-level constraints is related to the multidimensional knapsack problem (the main difference is that in the multidimensional knapsack the candidates can contribute more than a unit weight to each attribute-level constraint) and to the generic problem of optimising a submodular function subject to constraints (see, e.g., a survey by Krause and Golovin [37]). However, this literature usually deals with more general types of constraints, whereas the voting literature we discussed often concerns more specific approaches.

5.4 The Algorithmic Perspective on Strategic Voting

Other types of computational problems arise when one analyses how the results of ABC elections are affected by changes in voters' preferences. There are several reasons to study this type of computational problems, and we briefly summarise them below. Historically, the first motivation was to use the computational complexity as a shield protecting elections from strategic manipulations. The reasoning was the following: if we cannot construct a good rule that is strategyproof (e.g., due to known impossibility theorems; cf. Sect. 4.6), then we could at least aim at proposing a rule for which it is computationally hard for a voter to come up with a successful strategic manipulation. This motivation originated in the context of single-winner elections, and was first proposed by Bartholdi et al. [6]. This reasoning was later contested since the analysis of computational complexity is worst-case in spirit. Even for rules for which the problem of finding a successful strategic manipulation is NP-hard, such manipulations can be found easily in the average case, in particular for many real-life preference profiles. For a more detailed discussion of these arguments (but with a focus on single-winner elections), we refer the reader to a survey by Faliszewski and Procaccia [28], a book by Meir [45], and handbook chapters by Conitzer and Walsh [21] and Faliszewski and Rothe [29].

In addition to the original motivation to study strategic voting, there are other, more "positive" applications that do not concern insincere behaviour. For example, the question of whether one can stop eliciting preferences and safely determine the winners of an election is equivalent to asking whether a group of (undecided) voters can still change the outcome of an election. These questions are captured by the manipulation problems discussed in Sect. 5.4.1. Furthermore, the problem of deciding whether the result of an election is robust to small changes in the given preference profile can also be phrased as "bribing" voters to change their ballots so to change the election result. We discuss the robustness problem in Sect. 5.4.2.

Before we move further, we note that for the case of selecting a single winner ($k = 1$) under approval-based preferences, an excellent overview of computational issues related to strategic voting is given by Baumeister et al. [7].

5.4.1   Computational Complexity of Manipulation

We first consider the computational problem of finding a successful manipulation. Recall that we write A_{+X} to denote the profile A with one additional voter approving X, i.e., $A_{+X} = (A(1), \ldots, A(n), X)$.

Definition 5.1 Consider an ABC rule $\mathcal{R}$. In the UTILITY-MANIPULATION problem, we are given an election instance (A, k), a utility function $u \colon C \to \mathbb{R}$, and a threshold value $t \in \mathbb{R}$. We ask whether whether there exists a profile A' that extends A by r additional voters such that $\sum_{c \in W} u(c) \geq t$ for some $W \in \mathcal{R}(A_{+X}, k)$.

In the SUBSET-MANIPULATION problem, we are given an election (A, k), a subset of candidates $L \subseteq C$, and a positive integer r. We ask whether there exists a profile A' that extends A by r additional voters such that $L \subseteq W$ for some $W \in \mathcal{R}(A', k)$.

Intuitively, in UTILITY-MANIPULATION we have manipulators with a utility function describing their level of appreciation for different candidates; the utility function is additive. The question is whether the manipulators can submit approval ballots such that they derive a utility of at least t from the elected committee. In SUBSET-MANIPULATION, the goal is slightly different—the manipulators want to ensure that the candidates from a given set L are all selected. For $r = 1$, SUBSET-MANIPULATION can be represented as UTILITY-MANIPULATION: we assign the utility of one to the candidates from L and the utility of zero to the other candidates, and set $t = |L|$. Observe that it makes sense to consider UTILITY-MANIPULATION also in the context of AV—this is because AV is strategyproof only for approval preferences, while the definition of UTILITY-MANIPULATION assumes the manipulators have more fine-grained preferences.

Meir et al. [46] studied UTILITY-MANIPULATION for $r = 1$ and showed that it is solvable in polynomial time for Multi-Winner Approval Voting with adversarial tie-breaking,[4] Baumeister et al. [8] proved that also SUBSET-MANIPULATION is solvable in polynomial time for AV. (The main focus of both papers is on ranking-based multi-winner rules, cf. Sect. 6.1.) Aziz et al. [1] show that UTILITY-MANIPULATION is computationally hard for SAV and PAV with a given tie-breaking order on candidates. They further prove that SUBSET-MANIPULATION is NP-hard for SAV and coNP-hard for PAV. For PAV the problem stays hard even if there is only a single manipulator ($r = 1$), while for SAV with a single manipulator the problem becomes computable in polynomial time.

Bredereck et al. [11] studied a more general version of UTILITY-MANIPULATION, where the goal is to check whether there exists a coalition of voters that could jointly perform a successful manipulation. The authors focused on the ℓ-Bloc rule, which is a variant of Multi-Winner Approval Voting, where each voter approves exactly ℓ candidates. Then, the coalition-manipulation problem is computationally hard in its all variants studied by the authors. On the other hand, if we look at an egalitarian version of ℓ-Bloc (maximising the number of candidates in the committee that are approved by the worst-off voter), then the problem becomes computationally tractable. Another problem related to UTILITY-MANIPULATION has been considered by Barrot et al. [5]: given utility functions of all voters, is there an approval profile consistent with the utility functions in which a given committee wins.

5.4.2 Computational Complexity of Robustness

The next computational problem that we look at is ROBUSTNESS, introduced by Bredereck et al. [14] and adapted to the ABC setting by Gawron and Faliszewski [35]. In the definition below, we consider the following three operations: the operation Add adds a candidate to the approval set of some voter, Remove deletes a candidate from the approval set of a voter, and Swap is a combination of Add and Remove applied simultaneously to the approval set of a single voter.

Definition 5.2 (Bredereck et al. [14], Gawron and Faliszewski [35]) Consider an ABC rule $\mathcal{R}$ and an operation Op $\in$ {Add, Remove, Swap}. In the Op-ROBUSTNESS problem we are given an election instance (A, k) and an integer b. We ask whether there exist a sequence S of b operations of type Op such that $\mathcal{R}(A, k) \neq \mathcal{R}(A', k)$, where A' is the preference profile obtained from A by applying the operations from sequence S.

Gawron and Faliszewski [35] have shown that the Op-ROBUSTNESS problem is computationally hard for PAV and CC, for each type of the three operations. On the other hand, the problem can be solved in polynomial time for AV and SAV. The

---

[4] Adversarial tie-breaking means that ties between candidates are broken in disfavour of the manipulators.

authors also computed the robustness radius—a measure that says how much the result of an election can change in response to a single change in the preference profile—for several ABC rules. Notably, they show that for w-Thiele methods with $2w(1) > w(2)$ (this class includes PAV and CC), a single Add, Remove, or Swap operation can lead to a completely different winning committee.

Gawron and Faliszewski [35] and Misra and Sonar [47] also considered the parameterized complexity of the ROBUSTNESS problem, and have designed several parameterized algorithms for natural parameters, such as the number of voters n and the number of candidates m. Faliszewski et al. [31] considered a similar problem, but they asked whether, through a sequence of operations of a given type, one can make a particular candidate a member of a winning committee. This question is particularly relevant if one wants to report to non-winners how close they were to being selected. Finally, robustness of ABC rules has also been studied by Caragiannis et al. [19]; their analysis is based on a noise model assuming a "ground truth" (i.e., optimal) committee.

References

1. H. Aziz, S. Gaspers, J. Gudmundsson, S. Mackenzie, N. Mattei, and T. Walsh. Computational aspects of multi-winner approval voting. In *Proceedings of the 14th International Conference on Autonomous Agents and Multiagent Systems (AAMAS-2015)*, pages 107–115, 2015.
2. H. Aziz, M. Brill, V. Conitzer, E. Elkind, R. Freeman, and T. Walsh. Justified representation in approval-based committee voting. *Social Choice and Welfare*, 48(2):461–485, 2017.
3. H. Aziz, E. Elkind, S. Huang, M. Lackner, L. Sánchez-Fernández, and P. Skowron. On the complexity of extended and proportional justified representation. In *Proceedings of the 32nd Conference on Artificial Intelligence (AAAI-2018)*, pages 902–909, 2018.
4. S. Barman, O. Fawzi, S. Ghoshal, and E. Gürpınar. Tight approximation bounds for maximum multi-coverage. In *Proceedings of the 2020 International Conference on Integer Programming and Combinatorial Optimization (IPCO-2020)*, pages 66–77, 2020.
5. N. Barrot, L. Gourvès, J. Lang, J. Monnot, and B. Ries. Possible winners in approval voting. In *Proceedings of the 3rd International Conference on Algorithmic Decision Theory (ADT-2013)*, pages 57–70, 2013.
6. J. Bartholdi, III, C. Tovey, and M. Trick. The computational difficulty of manipulating an election. *Social Choice and Welfare*, 6(3):227–241, 1989.
7. D. Baumeister, G. Erdélyi, E. Hemaspaandra, L. Hemaspaandra, and J. Rothe. Computational aspects of approval voting. In J. F. Laslier and M. R. Sanver, editors, *Handbook of Approval Voting*, pages 199–251. Springer, 2010.
8. D. Baumeister, S. Dennisen, and L. Rey. Winner determination and manipulation in minisum and minimax committee elections. In *Proceedings of the 4th International Conference on Algorithmic Decision Theory (ADT-2015)*, pages 469–485, 2015.
9. N. Betzler, A. Slinko, and J. Uhlmann. On the computation of fully proportional representation. *Journal of Artificial Intelligence Research*, 47:475–519, 2013.
10. S. J. Brams. Constrained approval voting: A voting system to elect a governing board. *Interfaces*, 20(5):67–80, 1990.
11. R. Bredereck, A. Kaczmarczyk, and R. Niedermeier. On coalitional manipulation for multi-winner elections: Shortlisting. In *Proceedings of the 26th International Joint Conference on Artificial Intelligence (IJCAI-2017)*, pages 887–893, 2017.

12. R. Bredereck, P. Faliszewski, A. Igarashi, M. Lackner, and P. Skowron. Multiwinner elections with diversity constraints. In *Proceedings of the 32nd Conference on Artificial Intelligence (AAAI-2018)*, pages 933–940, 2018.
13. R. Bredereck, P. Faliszewski, A. Kaczmarczyk, D. Knop, and R. Niedermeier. Parameterized algorithms for finding a collective set of items. In *Proceedings of the 34th Conference on Artificial Intelligence (AAAI-2020)*, pages 1838–1845, 2020.
14. R. Bredereck, P. Faliszewski, A. Kaczmarczyk, R. Niedermeier, P. Skowron, and N. Talmon. Robustness among multiwinner voting rules. *Artificial Intelligence*, 290:103403, 2021.
15. M. Brill, R. Freeman, S. Janson, and M. Lackner. Phragmén's voting methods and justified representation. In *Proceedings of the 31st Conference on Artificial Intelligence (AAAI-2017)*, pages 406–413, 2017. Extended version at https://arxiv.org/abs/2102.12305.
16. J. Byrka and K. Sornat. PTAS for minimax approval voting. In *Proceedings of the 10th International Conference on Web and Internet Economics (WINE-2014)*, pages 203–217, 2014.
17. J. Byrka, P. Skowron, and K. Sornat. Proportional approval voting, harmonic k-median, and negative association. In *45th International Colloquium on Automata, Languages, and Programming, ICALP 2018*, volume 107 of *LIPIcs*, pages 26:1–26:14. Schloss Dagstuhl - Leibniz-Zentrum für Informatik, 2018.
18. I. Caragiannis, D. Kalaitzis, and E. Markakis. Approximation algorithms and mechanism design for minimax approval voting. In *Proceedings of the 24th Conference on Artificial Intelligence (AAAI-2010)*, pages 737–742, 2010.
19. I. Caragiannis, C. Kaklamanis, N. Karanikolas, and G. A. Krimpas. Evaluating approval-based multiwinner voting in terms of robustness to noise. *Autonomous Agents and Multi-Agent Systems*, 36(1):1–22, 2022.
20. L. E. Celis, L. Huang, and N. K. Vishnoi. Multiwinner voting with fairness constraints. In *Proceedings of the 27th International Joint Conference on Artificial Intelligence (IJCAI-2018)*, pages 144–151, 2018.
21. V. Conitzer and T. Walsh. Barriers to manipulation in voting. In F. Brandt, V. Conitzer, U. Endriss, J. Lang, and A. D. Procaccia, editors, *Handbook of Computational Social Choice*, pages 127–145. Cambridge University Press, New York, NY, USA, 1st edition, 2016.
22. M. Cygan, Ł. Kowalik, A. Socała, and K. Sornat. Approximation and parameterized complexity of minimax approval voting. *Journal of Artificial Intelligence Research*, 63:495–513, 2018.
23. F. Dietrich and C. List. Majority voting on restricted domains. *Journal of Economic Theory*, 145(2):512–543, 2010.
24. S. Dudycz, P. Manurangsi, J. Marcinkowski, and K. Sornat. Tight approximation for Proportional Approval Voting. In *Proceedings of the 29th International Joint Conference on Artificial Intelligence (IJCAI-2020)*, pages 276–282, 2020.
25. E. Elkind and M. Lackner. Structure in dichotomous preferences. In *Proceedings of the 24th International Joint Conference on Artificial Intelligence (IJCAI-2015)*, pages 2019–2025. ijcai.org, 2015.
26. E. Elkind, P. Faliszewski, M. Lackner, and S. Obraztsova. The complexity of recognizing incomplete single-crossing preferences. In *Proceedings of the 29th Conference on Artificial Intelligence (AAAI-2015)*, pages 865–871, 2015.
27. E. Elkind, M. Lackner, and D. Peters. Structured preferences. In U. Endriss, editor, *Trends in Computational Social Choice*, chapter 10, pages 187–207. AI Access, 2017.
28. P. Faliszewski and A. D. Procaccia. AI's war on manipulation: Are we winning? *AI Magazine*, 31(4):52–64, 2010.
29. P. Faliszewski and J. Rothe. Control and bribery in voting. In F. Brandt, V. Conitzer, U. Endriss, J. Lang, and A. D. Procaccia, editors, *Handbook of Computational Social Choice*, pages 146–168. Cambridge University Press, New York, NY, USA, 1st edition, 2016.
30. P. Faliszewski, E. Hemaspaandra, L. Hemaspaandra, and J. Rothe. The shield that never was: Societies with single-peaked preferences are more open to manipulation and control. *Information and Computation*, 209(2):89–107, 2011.
31. P. Faliszewski, P. Skowron, and N. Talmon. Bribery as a measure of candidate success: Complexity results for approval-based multiwinner rules. In *Proceedings of the 16th International Conference on Autonomous Agents and Multiagent Systems (AAMAS-2017)*, pages 6–14, 2017.

32. P. Faliszewski, P. Skowron, A. Slinko, and N. Talmon. Multiwinner analogues of the plurality rule: Axiomatic and algorithmic views. *Social Choice and Welfare*, 51(3):513–550, 2018.
33. Z. Fitzsimmons and M. Lackner. Incomplete preferences in single-peaked electorates. *Journal of Artificial Intelligence Research*, 67:797–833, 2020.
34. T. Gavenčiak, M. Koutecký, and D. Knop. Integer programming in parameterized complexity: Five miniatures. *Discrete Optimization*, page 100596, 2020.
35. G. Gawron and P. Faliszewski. Robustness of approval-based multiwinner voting rules. In *Proceedings of the 6th International Conference on Algorithmic Decision Theory (ADT-2019)*, pages 17–31, 2019.
36. M. Godziszewski, P. Batko, P. Skowron, and P. Faliszewski. An analysis of approval-based committee rules for 2D-Euclidean elections. In *Proceedings of the 35th Conference on Artificial Intelligence (AAAI-2021)*, pages 5448–5455, 2021.
37. A. Krause and D. Golovin. Submodular function maximization. Technical report, 2012.
38. M. Lackner, P. Regner, B. Krenn, and S. S. Forster. abcvoting: A Python library of approval-based committee voting rules, 2021. URL https://doi.org/10.5281/zenodo.3904466. Current version: https://github.com/martinlackner/abcvoting.
39. J. Lang and P. Skowron. Multi-attribute proportional representation. *Artificial Intelligence*, 263:74–106, 2018.
40. R. LeGrand, E. Markakis, and A. Mehta. Some results on approximating the minimax solution in approval voting. In *Proceedings of the 6th International Conference on Autonomous Agents and Multiagent Systems (AAMAS-2007)*, pages 198:1–198:3, 2007.
41. H. W. Lenstra. Integer programming with a fixed number of variables. *Mathematics of Operations Research*, 8(4):538–548, 1983.
42. C. List. A possibility theorem on aggregation over multiple interconnected propositions. *Mathematical Social Sciences*, 45(1):1–13, 2003.
43. H. Liu and J. Guo. Parameterized complexity of winner determination in minimax committee elections. In *Proceedings of the 15th International Conference on Autonomous Agents and Multiagent Systems (AAMAS-2016)*, pages 341–349, 2016.
44. T. Lu and C. Boutilier. Budgeted social choice: From consensus to personalized decision making. In *Proceedings of the 22nd International Joint Conference on Artificial Intelligence (IJCAI-2011)*, pages 280–286, 2011.
45. R. Meir. *Strategic voting*. Synthesis Lectures on Artificial Intelligence and Machine Learning. Morgan & Claypool Publishers, 2018.
46. R. Meir, A. D. Procaccia, J. S. Rosenschein, and A. Zohar. Complexity of strategic behavior in multi-winner elections. *Journal of Artificial Intelligence Research*, 33:149–178, 2008.
47. N. Misra and C. Sonar. Robustness radius for Chamberlin-Courant on restricted domains. In *Proceedings of the 45th International Conference on Current Trends in Theory and Practice of Computer Science (SOFSEM-2019)*, pages 341–353, 2019.
48. N. Misra, A. Nabeel, and H. Singh. On the parameterized complexity of minimax approval voting. In *Proceedings of the 14th International Conference on Autonomous Agents and Multiagent Systems (AAMAS-2015)*, pages 97–105, 2015.
49. G. Nemhauser, L. Wolsey, and M. Fisher. An analysis of approximations for maximizing submodular set functions. *Mathematical Programming*, 14(1):265–294, 1978.
50. D. Peters. Recognising multidimensional Euclidean preferences. In *Proceedings of the 31st Conference on Artificial Intelligence (AAAI-2017)*, pages 642–648, 2017.
51. D. Peters and M. Lackner. Preferences single-peaked on a circle. *Journal of Artificial Intelligence Research*, 68:463–502, 2020.
52. D. Peters and P. Skowron. Proportionality and the limits of welfarism. In *Proceedings of the 2020 ACM Conference on Economics and Computation (ACM-EC-2020)*, pages 793–794, 2020. Extended version at https://arxiv.org/abs/1911.11747.
53. R. Potthoff. Use of linear programming for constrained approval voting. *Interfaces*, 20(5):79–80, 1990.
54. R. F. Potthoff and S. J. Brams. Proportional representation: Broadening the options. *Journal of Theoretical Politics*, 10(2):147–178, 1998.

55. A. D. Procaccia, J. S. Rosenschein, and A. Zohar. On the complexity of achieving proportional representation. *Social Choice and Welfare*, 30(3):353–362, 2008.

56. L. Sánchez-Fernández, E. Elkind, M. Lackner, N. Fernández, J. A. Fisteus, P. Basanta Val, and P. Skowron. Proportional justified representation. In *Proceedings of the 31st Conference on Artificial Intelligence (AAAI-2017)*, pages 670–676, 2017.

57. P. Skowron. FPT approximation schemes for maximizing submodular functions. *Information and Computation*, 257:65–78, 2017.

58. P. Skowron and P. Faliszewski. Chamberlin-Courant rule with approval ballots: Approximating the maxcover problem with bounded frequencies in FPT time. *Journal of Artificial Intelligence Research*, 60:687–716, 2017.

59. P. Skowron, P. Faliszewski, and J. Lang. Finding a collective set of items: From proportional multirepresentation to group recommendation. *Artificial Intelligence*, 241:191–216, 2016.

60. P. Skowron, M. Lackner, M. Brill, D. Peters, and E. Elkind. Proportional rankings. In *Proceedings of the 26th International Joint Conference on Artificial Intelligence (IJCAI-2017)*, pages 409–415, 2017.

61. A. Straszak, M. Libura, J. Sikorski, and D. Wagner. Computer-assisted constrained approval voting. *Group Decision and Negotiation*, 2(4):375–385, 1993.

62. Z. Terzopoulou, A. Karpov, and S. Obraztsova. Restricted domains of dichotomous preferences with possibly incomplete information. In *Proceedings of the 19th International Conference on Autonomous Agents and Multiagent Systems (AAMAS-2020)*, pages 2023–2025, 2020.

63. Y. Yang. On the tree representations of dichotomous preferences. In *Proceedings of the 28th International Joint Conference on Artificial Intelligence (IJCAI-2019)*, pages 10–16, 2019.

64. Y. Yang and J. Wang. Parameterized complexity of multi-winner determination: More effort towards fixed-parameter tractability. In *Proceedings of the 17th International Conference on Autonomous Agents and Multiagent Systems (AAMAS-2018)*, pages 2142–2144, 2018.

Chapter 6
Related Formalisms and Applications

In this chapter, we discuss connections of approval-based committee voting with a number of other applications and formalisms.

6.1 Ranking-Based Multi-Winner Elections

Besides ABC voting, the other classic multi-winner election model is when voters provide a ranking of candidates from the most to the least preferred one. That is, in the ranking-based model a voter's preference is expressed as a linear order of all candidates instead of a subset of candidates, as it is the case in the ABC model. As it is the case with approval-based multi-winner elections, also the ranking-based model has attracted much attention in recent years. Alas, at the point of writing this book, there does not exist a comprehensive overview of this field of research. However, a very helpful introduction to multi-winner voting in general (with a focus on the ranking-based model) can found in a book chapter by Faliszewski et al. [32].

When comparing approval-based and ranking-based multi-winner rules, it is worth mentioning that the class of ABC scoring rules (Definition 3.5) has a very close analogue in the ranking-based model, namely the class of committee scoring rules [28]. Indeed, committee scoring rules admit a very similar axiomatic characterisation to the one given in Theorem 3.2 for ABC scoring rules [64]. The class of committee scoring rules has been explored in depth by Faliszewski et al. [33]. In particular, the subclass of OWA-based committee scoring rules corresponds to the class of Thiele methods in the approval-based model. Other subclasses of committee scoring rules can be analogously defined for approval ballots, but to the best of our knowledge they have not been considered in the context of approval-based elections.

The approval-based and ranking-based model can be generalised to the model where voters provide weak orders over candidates, i.e., ranking with ties. In this model, approval ballots correspond to a ranking with two levels (approved and dis-

© The Author(s) 2023
M. Lackner and P. Skowron, *Multi-Winner Voting with Approval Preferences*,
SpringerBriefs in Intelligent Systems, https://doi.org/10.1007/978-3-031-09016-5_6

approved candidates). This variant has been considered, e.g., by Aziz and Lee [4], but generally attracted much less attention so far. This is due to the fact that the concepts discussed in this book (e.g., notions of proportionality) do not easily generalise to this more expressive setting and require substantial conceptual developments. Further work is required to consolidate the literature from the approval-based and ranking-based model in a systematic and notationally concise form.

6.2   Trichotomous Preferences and Incomplete Information

In this book we consider the variant of the multi-winner election model where agents vote by specifying sets of approved candidates. Several recent (mostly algorithmic) works study an extended variant of this model, where the ballots are trichotomous, i.e., where each voter can approve, disapprove or remain neutral with regard to a candidate. This model is discussed in detail by Brams and Fishburn [17] and Lines [56]. Baumeister and Dennisen [10] and Baumeister et al. [11] generalise AV and MAV to trichotomous votes and explore related algorithmic questions. This line of work has been continued by Liu and Guo [58]. Further, Baumeister et al. [12] extend MAV to the case where each voter assigns each candidate to one of ℓ predefined buckets, where ℓ is a parameter. Zhou et al. [68] introduce variants of CC, PAV, and SAV for trichotomous ballots and study questions regarding parameterized complexity. Finally, Talmon and Page [66] define and study notions of proportionality in the trichotomous setting. In general, many questions regarding the trichotomous model remain unanswered. In particular, an axiomatic analysis is mostly missing (with work of Alcantud and Laruelle [1] and Gonzalez et al. [40] as notable exceptions).

A model closely related to trichotomous preferences arises if approval ballots are incomplete due to missing information. In this model, the middle, "neutral" option corresponds to "unknown". In practice, voting rules often have to be computed given incomplete information (such as missing ballots or incomplete ballots; see the handbook chapter of Boutilier and Rosenschein [16] for a broader discussion). For ABC rules, a first analysis with focus on AV is due to Barrot et al. [9]. A more comprehensive treatment by Imber et al. [45] considers the class of Thiele methods and focuses on computational problems related to incomplete information. Apart from the three-valued model of incomplete information, as discussed here, they also propose models where "unknown" candidates are ordered by preference but it is unclear where to separate them in approved and disapproved candidates. Finally, Terzopoulou et al. [67] study structured preference domains (cf. Sect. 5.2.4) in connection with incomplete information.

6.3 A Variable Number of Winners

Throughout this paper, we assume that the committee size is fixed. In the literature on multi-winner voting with a variable number of winners [48, 49] (also known as *social dichotomy functions* [26]), this assumption is dropped and a voting rule can return an arbitrary number of candidates—depending on the given election instance. An example for such a rule, based on approval ballots, is the *mean rule*, which returns all candidates with an above-average number of approvals (introduced by Duddy et al. [27], further analysed by Brandl and Peters [19]). Another example is Minimax Approval Voting (MAV), as discussed in Sect. 2.7. In this setting, MAV returns all candidate subsets that minimise the largest Hamming distance among all voters. Other ABC rules do not easily translate to this setting. For example, Thiele methods always achieve a maximum score for the complete set of all alternatives. Consequently, the formulation of such voting rules often contains a penalty mechanism for larger sets.

More details, in particular a computational view point and an experimental evaluation, can be found in the work of Faliszewski et al. [34]. Further, the special case of shortlisting rules has been analysed by Lackner and Maly [54]; this work includes recommendations which voting rules are particularly suitable for shortlisting scenarios. Shortlisting in a proportional fashion was studied by Freeman et al. [36]; their focus lies on proportionality guarantees (related to the ones introduced in Sect. 4.2) for variable-sized sets of candidates. Finally, Allouche et al. [2] consider an epistemic scenario where a "correct" selection of candidates has to be identified; approval ballots are viewed as noisy estimates of a ground truth.

6.4 Participatory Budgeting

In participatory budgeting (PB), we assume that candidates come with different costs, and that the sum of the costs of the selected candidates cannot exceed a given budget. Thus, multi-winner elections can be viewed as a special case of PB, where the costs of the candidates are all equal. Typically, candidates correspond to projects in this setting, each of which has an associated cost to be implemented. For an overview of different models and approaches to PB, we refer the reader to a recent survey by Aziz and Shah [5].

Participatory budgeting based on approval ballots is one of the standard models and is often used in real-world PB referenda. Knapsack voting suggested by Goel et al. [39] closely resembles AV. Peters et al. [60] showed that the Method of Equal Shares preserves its proportionality properties in the setting of PB—it satisfies an adapted version of EJR, and a logarithmic approximation of the core. Aziz et al. [6] provide a taxonomy of axioms aimed at formalising proportionality in PB; those axioms are adaptations of JR and PJR (see Sect. 4.2). Talmon and Faliszewski [65] study other axioms, mostly pertaining to different forms of monotonicity (see Sects.

3.3 and 3.4) and through experiments provide visualisations of the kind of committees returned by different participatory budgeting rules. Baumeister et al. [13] consider the computational complexity of strategic voting. Generally, the assumption is that projects are independent of each other; Jain et al. [47] study participatory budgeting without this assumption. Finally, Rey et al. [61] connect participatory budgeting based on approval ballots with judgement aggregation (see Sect. 6.7), which offers another possibility to include constraints.

6.5 Budget Division and Probabilistic Social Choice

The goal of a probabilistic social choice function is to divide a single unit of a global resource between the candidates. Thus, multi-winner elections can be viewed as instances of probabilistic social choice with the additional requirement that each candidate gets either 1/k-th fraction of the global resource, or nothing. For an overview of results on probabilistic social choice functions, we refer to a book chapter by Brandt [21].

Several works [7, 15, 20, 25, 31, 59] study probabilistic social choice functions for approval votes. The particular focus of some of these works is put on formalising the concepts of fairness and proportionality. Some of these concepts closely resemble the ones that we discussed in the context of approval-based multi-winner elections (Sect. 4). For example, Aziz et al. [7] and Fain et al. [31] study the concept of the core (Sect. 4.4), Aziz et al. [7] additionally consider the axioms of average fair share, group fair share, and individual fair share—the properties that closely resemble— respectively—proportionality degree, PJR, and JR (Sect. 4.2), Michorzewski et al. [59] show the relation between these fairness properties and the utilitarian welfare of outcomes (cf. Sect. 4.5.2). Bogomolnaia et al. [15] focuses on mechanisms which are strategyproof, and Duddy [25] proves that strategyproofness is incompatible with certain forms of proportionality—an impossibility result similar to the ones that we discuss in Sect. 4.6.

6.6 Voting in Combinatorial Domains

Multi-winner rules output fixed-size subsets of available candidates. An alternative way of thinking of such rules is that (1) for each candidate c they make a decision whether c should be selected to the winning committee or not, and (2) there is a constraint which specifies that exactly k decisions must be positive. Thus, with m candidates there are m dependent binary decisions (each decision is of the form "include a candidate in the winning committee or not") that are made by a multi-winner rule. These decisions are dependent (related) because of the constraint on the number of positive decisions.

The literature on voting in combinatorial domains studies a more general setup, where a number of decisions (not necessarily binary) need to be made, and where there exist (possibly complex) relations between the decisions. Similarly, the preferences of the voters might have complex forms. For example, consider two issues—I_1 with two possible decisions Y_1 and N_1, and I_2 with two possible decisions Y_2 and N_2. A voter might prefer decision Y_2 only if the decision with respect to issue I_1 is Y_1; otherwise this voter might prefer N_2 over Y_2 (see the work of Brams et al. [18] for a detailed discussion of this example). Various languages have been studied that allow voters to express such complex combinatorial preferences. For example, in the context of approval-based multi-winner elections, some of these languages would allow voters to express the view that a certain group of candidates works particularly well together, so they should either be all selected as members of the winning committee or none of them should be chosen, or the view that some candidates should never be chosen together. In the literature on multi-winner elections, on the other hand, it is assumed that the preferences of the voters are separable, thus the voters can only make statements about their levels of appreciation for different candidates. An interesting middle ground between very general forms of combinatorial preferences and simple (i.e., separable) preferences was proposed by Barrot and Lang [8]: conditional approval ballots allow voters to specify their approval ballots conditional on whether certain candidates are to be included in the committee.

A comprehensive overview of the literature on voting in combinatorial domains can be found in a book chapter by Lang and Xia [55]. We highlight three works from this literature that deal with models particularly related to the model of approval-based multi-winner elections. In public decision making, as studied by Conitzer et al. [23], the decisions are not related, the preferences of the voters with respect to decisions on various issues are separable, thus the model closely resembles the one studied in this book. The main difference is that in the model for public decisions there is no constraint specifying the number of decisions that can be positive. There, the authors focus on designing fair (i.e., proportional) rules. The model of sub-committee elections, due to Aziz and Lee [3], generalises the ones of multi-winner elections and public decisions. There, it is assumed that the set of candidates is partitioned and for each group of candidates there is a threshold bounding the number of candidates selected from this group.

Another formalism closely related to ABC voting is *perpetual voting*, introduced by Lackner [53]. Here, instead of a committee we have time steps and in each step one candidate is selected. Hence, after k rounds k candidates are picked, which can be viewed as a committee. The main difference is that the set of available candidates and voters' preferences can change each round. The goal is to provide proportionality over time, which requires that the decision in round k is made under consideration of the voters' satisfaction in previous rounds. This formalism can be viewed as a special case of voting in combinatorial domains (with a very specific sequentiality constraint). Further, due to the sequential structure imposed by time, perpetual voting rules have close connections with committee monotonic ABC rules (such as seq-Phragmén and seq-PAV). Similar questions in a utility-based model have been studied by Freeman et al. [35]. A voting rule related to the setting of perpetual voting is due to Gottlob

Frege[1] [37, 38]. The main difference is that the set of candidates remains the same in each round and the goal is to achieve a proportionally fair outcome for candidates (instead of voters). An analysis of this voting system is due to Harrenstein et al. [44].

6.7   Judgment Aggregation and Propositional Belief Merging

In judgment aggregation, we are given a set of logical propositions and a set of voters providing true/false valuations for these propositions; the goal is to find a collective, aggregated valuation. Sometimes it is also required that the collective valuation must be consistent with exogenous logical constraints. Multi-winner elections can be represented as instances of judgment aggregation, where for each candidate we have a single Boolean variable representing whether the candidate is elected or not; the exogenous constraints can be used to enforce that exactly k from these variables are set true. A chapter by Endriss [29] in the *Handbook of Computational Social Choice* discusses this framework in detail and reviews judgment aggregation rules; see also the survey by List and Puppe [57].

Propositional belief merging [50–52] is a very general framework, which allows agents to aggregate their individual positions (beliefs, preferences, judgements, goals) on a set of issues. Also here this combined, collective outcome has to satisfy given exogenous logical constraints. Approval-based committee voting can be seen as a special case of propositional belief merging, although the focus of these two directions of research has little overlap: belief merging operators are analysed with respect to a set of postulates that are only partially relevant in a voting context. A few works have made an explicit effort to connect voting and belief merging. A particular focus in this regard has been the study of belief merging and strategyproofness [22, 30, 41]. Further, Haret et al. [42] consider classic axioms from social choice theory in the context of belief merging. Finally, Haret et al. [43] introduce and analysed *proportional* belief merging operators.

6.8   Proportional Rankings

The theory of multi-winner elections can be applied in a seemingly unrelated setting, where the goal is to find a ranking of candidates based on voters' preferences. One can observe that every committee monotonic (Definition 3.2), resolute ABC rule $\mathcal{R}$ can be used to obtain a ranking of candidates: we put in the first position in the ranking the candidate that $\mathcal{R}$ returns for $k = 1$; call this candidate c. Committee monotonicity guarantees that the set of two candidates returned by $\mathcal{R}$ for $k = 2$ contains c; the other candidate is put in the second position in the ranking, etc.

---

[1] Gottlob Frege (1848–1925) was a German philosopher and logician.

In particular, if we use a proportional committee-monotonic rule (for example, seq-Phragmén or seq-PAV) then the obtained ranking will proportionally reflect the views of the voters in the sense that each prefix of such a ranking, viewed as a committee, will be proportional; this idea has been studied in detail by Skowron et al. [63]. Proportional rankings are desirable, e.g., when one wants to provide a list of recommendations or search results that accommodate different types of users (cf. *diversifying search results* [24, 62]), or in the context of liquid democracy [14], where an ordered list of proposals is presented to voters for their consideration.

Proportional rankings in a dynamic setting, where the rankings also take previously selected (and now unavailable) alternatives into account, have been studied by Israel and Brill [46]. This setting arises, e.g., in dynamic Q&A platforms, where questions are proposed and upvoted. The authors argue that questions that already have been asked should be taken into account when choosing the next question(s).

References

1. J. C. R. Alcantud and A. Laruelle. Dis&approval voting: a characterization. *Social Choice and Welfare*, 43(1):1–10, 2014.
2. T. Allouche, J. Lang, and F. Yger. Multi-winner approval voting goes epistemic. *CoRR*, abs/2201.06655, 2022. URL https://arxiv.org/abs/2201.06655.
3. H. Aziz and B. E. Lee. Sub-committee approval voting and generalized justified representation axioms. In *Proceedings of the 2018 AAAI/ACM Conference on AI, Ethics, and Society*, pages 3–9, 2018.
4. H. Aziz and B. E. Lee. The expanding approvals rule: Improving proportional representation and monotonicity. *Social Choice and Welfare*, 54(1):1–45, 2020.
5. H. Aziz and N. Shah. Participatory budgeting: Models and approaches. In *Pathways Between Social Science and Computational Social Science*, pages 215–236. Springer, 2021.
6. H. Aziz, B. E. Lee, and N. Talmon. Proportionally representative participatory budgeting: Axioms and algorithms. In *Proceedings of the 16th International Conference on Autonomous Agents and Multiagent Systems (AAMAS-2017)*, pages 23–31, 2018.
7. H. Aziz, A. Bogomolnaia, and H. Moulin. Fair mixing: the case of dichotomous preferences. In *Proceedings of the 2019 ACM Conference on Economics and Computation (ACM-EC-2019)*, pages 753–781, 2019.
8. N. Barrot and J. Lang. Conditional and sequential approval voting on combinatorial domains. In *Proceedings of the 25th International Joint Conference on Artificial Intelligence (IJCAI-2016)*, pages 88–94, 2016.
9. N. Barrot, L. Gourvès, J. Lang, J. Monnot, and B. Ries. Possible winners in approval voting. In *Proceedings of the 3rd International Conference on Algorithmic Decision Theory (ADT-2013)*, pages 57–70, 2013.
10. D. Baumeister and S. Dennisen. Voter dissatisfaction in committee elections. In *Proceedings of the 14th International Conference on Autonomous Agents and Multiagent Systems (AAMAS-2015)*, pages 1707–1708, 2015.
11. D. Baumeister, S. Dennisen, and L. Rey. Winner determination and manipulation in minisum and minimax committee elections. In *Proceedings of the 4th International Conference on Algorithmic Decision Theory (ADT-2015)*, pages 469–485, 2015.
12. D. Baumeister, T. Böhnlein, L. Rey, O. Schaudt, and A. Selker. Minisum and minimax committee election rules for general preference types. In *Proceedings of the 22nd European Conference on Artificial Intelligence (ECAI-2016)*, pages 1656–1657, 2016.

13. D. Baumeister, L. Boes, and J. Hillebrand. Complexity of manipulative interference in participatory budgeting. In *Proceedings of the 7th International Conference on Algorithmic Decision Theory (ADT-2021)*, volume 13023 of *Lecture Notes in Computer Science*, pages 424–439. Springer, 2021.

14. J. Behrens, A. Kistner, A. Nitsche, and B. Swierczek. *The Principles of LiquidFeedback*. Interaktive Demokratie e.V. Berlin, 2014.

15. A. Bogomolnaia, H. Moulin, and R. Stong. Collective choice under dichotomous preferences. *Journal of Economic Theory*, 122(2):165–184, 2005.

16. C. Boutilier and J. S. Rosenschein. Incomplete information and communication in voting. In F. Brandt, V. Conitzer, U. Endriss, J. Lang, and A. Procaccia, editors, *Handbook of Computational Social Choice*. Cambridge University Press, 2016.

17. S. J. Brams and P. C. Fishburn. Approval voting. *American Political Science Review*, 72(3):831–847, 1978.

18. S. J. Brams, D. M. Kilgour, and W. Zwicker. Voting on referenda: the separability problem and possible solutions. *Electoral Studies*, 16(3):359–377, 1997.

19. F. Brandl and D. Peters. An axiomatic characterization of the Borda mean rule. *Social choice and welfare*, 52(4):685–707, 2019.

20. F. Brandl, F. Brandt, D. Peters, C. Stricker, and W. Suksompong. Funding public projects: A case for the Nash product rule, 2020. Working paper.

21. F. Brandt. Rolling the dice: Recent results in probabilistic social choice. In U. Endriss, editor, *Trends in Computational Social Choice*, chapter 1, pages 3–26. AI Access, 2017.

22. S. Chopra, A. Ghose, and T. Meyer. Social choice theory, belief merging, and strategy-proofness. *Information Fusion*, 7(1):61–79, 2006.

23. V. Conitzer, R. Freeman, and N. Shah. Fair public decision making. In *Proceedings of the 2017 ACM Conference on Economics and Computation*, pages 629–646, 2017.

24. M. Drosou and E. Pitoura. Search result diversification. *ACM SIGMOD Record*, 39(1):41–47, 2010.

25. C. Duddy. Fair sharing under dichotomous preferences. *Mathematical Social Sciences*, 73:1–5, 2015.

26. C. Duddy, N. Houy, J. Lang, A. Piggins, and W. S. Zwicker. Social dichotomy functions. Extended abstract for presentation at the 2014 meeting of the Society for Social Choice and Welfare, 2014.

27. C. Duddy, A. Piggins, and W. S. Zwicker. Aggregation of binary evaluations: a borda-like approach. *Social Choice and Welfare*, 46(2):301–333, 2016.

28. E. Elkind, P. Faliszewski, P. Skowron, and A. Slinko. Properties of multiwinner voting rules. *Social Choice and Welfare*, 48(3):599–632, 2017.

29. U. Endriss. Judgment aggregation. In F. Brandt, V. Conitzer, U. Endriss, J. Lang, and A. D. Procaccia, editors, *Handbook of Computational Social Choice*, pages 399–426. Cambridge University Press, New York, NY, USA, 1st edition, 2016.

30. P. Everaere, S. Konieczny, and P. Marquis. The strategy-proofness landscape of merging. *Journal of Artificial Intelligence Research*, 28:49–105, 2007.

31. B. Fain, A. Goel, and K. Munagala. The core of the participatory budgeting problem. In *Proceedings of the 12th International Conference on Web and Internet Economics (WINE-2016)*, pages 384–399, 2016.

32. P. Faliszewski, P. Skowron, A. Slinko, and N. Talmon. Multiwinner voting: A new challenge for social choice theory. In U. Endriss, editor, *Trends in Computational Social Choice*, chapter 2, pages 27–47. AI Access, 2017.

33. P. Faliszewski, P. Skowron, A. Slinko, and N. Talmon. Committee scoring rules: Axiomatic characterization and hierarchy. *ACM Transactions on Economics and Computation*, 6(1):Article 3, 2019.

34. P. Faliszewski, A. Slinko, and N. Talmon. Multiwinner rules with variable number of winners. In *Proceedings of the 24th European Conference on Artificial Intelligence (ECAI-2020)*, pages 67–74, 2020. URL https://doi.org/10.3233/FAIA200077.

35. R. Freeman, S. M. Zahedi, and V. Conitzer. Fair and efficient social choice in dynamic settings. In *Proceedings of the 26th International Joint Conference on Artificial Intelligence (IJCAI-2017)*, pages 4580–4587. ijcai.org, 2017.

36. R. Freeman, A. Kahng, and D. M. Pennock. Proportionality in approval-based elections with a variable number of winners. In *Proceedings of the 29th International Joint Conference on Artificial Intelligence (IJCAI-2020)*, pages 132–138, 2020.

37. G. Frege. Vorschläge für ein Wahlgesetz. Original typescript at the Thüringer Universitäts- und Landesbibliothek (ThULB), 1918. URL https://archive.thulb.uni-jena.de/collections/receive/HisBest_cbu_00022979.

38. G. Frege. Vorschläge für ein Wahlgesetz. In G. Gabriel and U. Dathe, editors, *Gottlob Frege: Werk und Wirkung. Mit den unveröffentlichten Vorschlägen für ein Wahlgesetz von Gottlob Frege*, pages 297–313. Mentis, 2000.

39. A. Goel, A. K. Krishnaswamy, S. Sakshuwong, and T. Aitamurto. Knapsack voting. *Collective Intelligence*, 1, 2015.

40. S. Gonzalez, A. Laruelle, and P. Solal. Dilemma with approval and disapproval votes. *Social Choice and Welfare*, 53(3):497–517, 2019.

41. A. Haret and J. P. Wallner. Manipulating skeptical and credulous consequences when merging beliefs. In *European Conference on Logics in Artificial Intelligence (JELIA-2019)*, pages 133–150, 2019.

42. A. Haret, A. Pfandler, and S. Woltran. Beyond IC postulates: Classification criteria for merging operators. In *ECAI*, pages 372–380, 2016.

43. A. Haret, M. Lackner, A. Pfandler, and J. P. Wallner. Proportional belief merging. In *Proceedings of the 34th AAAI Conference on Artificial Intelligence (AAAI 2020)*, pages 2822–2829, 2020.

44. P. Harrenstein, M.-L. Lackner, and M. Lackner. A mathematical analysis of an election system proposed by Gottlob Frege. *Erkenntnis*, 2020.

45. A. Imber, J. Israel, M. Brill, and B. Kimelfeld. Committee voting with incomplete approvals. *CoRR*, abs/2103.14847, 2021. URL https://arxiv.org/abs/2103.14847.

46. J. Israel and M. Brill. Dynamic proportional rankings. In *Proceedings of the 30th International Joint Conference on Artificial Intelligence (IJCAI-2021)*, pages 261–267, 2021.

47. P. Jain, K. Sornat, and N. Talmon. Participatory budgeting with project interactions. In *Proceedings of the 29th International Joint Conference on Artificial Intelligence (IJCAI-2020)*, pages 386–392. ijcai.org, 2020.

48. D. M. Kilgour. Approval balloting for multi-winner elections. In J.-F. Laslier and M. R. Sanver, editors, *Handbook on Approval Voting*, pages 105–124. Springer, 2010.

49. D. M. Kilgour. Approval elections with a variable number of winners. *Theory and Decision*, 81, 02 2016.

50. S. Konieczny and R. Pino Pérez. Merging information under constraints: A logical framework. *Journal of Logic and Computation*, 12(5):773–808, 2002.

51. S. Konieczny and R. Pino Pérez. Logic based merging. *Journal of Philosophical Logic*, 40(2):239–270, 2011.

52. S. Konieczny, J. Lang, and P. Marquis. DA^2 merging operators. *Artificial Intelligence*, 157(1-2):49–79, 2004.

53. M. Lackner. Perpetual voting: Fairness in long-term decision making. In *Proceedings of the 34th AAAI Conference on Artificial Intelligence (AAAI 2020)*, pages 2103–2110, 2020.

54. M. Lackner and J. Maly. Approval-based shortlisting. In *Proceedings of the 20th International Conference on Autonomous Agents and Multiagent Systems (AAMAS-2021)*, pages 1566–1568, 2021.

55. J. Lang and L. Xia. Voting in combinatorial domains. In F. Brandt, V. Conitzer, U. Endriss, J. Lang, and A. D. Procaccia, editors, *Handbook of Computational Social Choice*. Cambridge University Press, 2016.

56. M. Lines. Approval voting and strategy analysis: A venetian example. *Theory and Decision*, 20(2):155–172, 1986.

57. C. List and C. Puppe. Judgment aggregation: A survey. In P. Anand, P. Pattanaik, and C. Puppe, editors, *The Handbook of Rational and Social Choice*. Oxford University Press, 2009.
58. H. Liu and J. Guo. Parameterized complexity of winner determination in minimax committee elections. In *Proceedings of the 15th International Conference on Autonomous Agents and Multiagent Systems (AAMAS-2016)*, pages 341–349, 2016.
59. M. Michorzewski, D. Peters, and P. Skowron. Price of fairness in budget division and probabilistic social choice. In *Proceedings of the 34th Conference on Artificial Intelligence (AAAI-2020)*, pages 2184–2191, 2020.
60. D. Peters, G. Pierczynski, and P. Skowron. Proportional participatory budgeting with additive utilities. In *Proceedings of the Thirty-fifth Conference on Neural Information Processing Systems (NeurIPS-2021)*, pages 12726–12737, 2021.
61. S. Rey, U. Endriss, and R. de Haan. Designing participatory budgeting mechanisms grounded in judgment aggregation. In *Proceedings of the 17th International Conference on Principles of Knowledge Representation and Reasoning, (KR-2020)*, pages 692–702, 2020.
62. R. L. T. Santos, C. MacDonald, and I. Ounis. Search result diversification. *Foundations and Trends in Information Retrieval*, 9(1):1–90, 2015.
63. P. Skowron, M. Lackner, M. Brill, D. Peters, and E. Elkind. Proportional rankings. In *Proceedings of the 26th International Joint Conference on Artificial Intelligence (IJCAI-2017)*, pages 409–415, 2017.
64. P. Skowron, P. Faliszewski, and A. Slinko. Axiomatic characterization of committee scoring rules. *Journal of Economic Theory*, 180:244–273, 2019.
65. N. Talmon and P. Faliszewski. A framework for approval-based budgeting methods. In *Proceedings of the 33rd Conference on Artificial Intelligence (AAAI-2019)*, volume 33, pages 2181–2188, 2019.
66. N. Talmon and R. Page. Proportionality in committee selection with negative feelings. *CoRR*, abs/2101.01435, 2021. URL https://arxiv.org/abs/2101.01435.
67. Z. Terzopoulou, A. Karpov, and S. Obraztsova. Restricted domains of dichotomous preferences with possibly incomplete information. In *Proceedings of the 19th International Conference on Autonomous Agents and Multiagent Systems (AAMAS-2020)*, pages 2023–2025, 2020.
68. A. Zhou, Y. Yang, and J. Guo. Parameterized complexity of committee elections with dichotomous and trichotomous votes. In *Proceedings of the 18th International Conference on Autonomous Agents and Multiagent Systems (AAMAS-2019)*, pages 503–510, 2019.

Chapter 7
Outlook and Research Directions

We conclude this book with a list of what we view as particularly important open problems and research directions. This is followed by a list of more specific or more technical open questions. These two lists are naturally far from being exhaustive; many more research directions remain to be explored.

7.1 Main Open Problems and Research Questions

Q1 **Axiomatic characterisations**: So far, only few axiomatic characterisations of ABC rules are known. Specifically, such characterisations are known only for ABC scoring rules and Thiele methods. Yet, axiomatic characterisations are essential if one wants to choose an ABC rule in a principled way. It is thus one of the major open problems to characterise other ABC rules, in particular, sequential Thiele methods, seq-Phragmén, the Method of Equal Shares, Monroe's rule, Minimax Approval Voting, and Satisfaction Approval Voting. Further, almost no satisfiable proportionality-related axioms are known for the multi-attribute model (Sect. 4.7), let alone axiomatic characterisations.

Q2 **Committee monotonicity and proportionality**: The current state of research suggests that committee monotonic ABC rules are limited in how proportional they are, but there is no precise impossibility result known as of now. The main open question is whether there exist ABC rules that satisfy EJR and committee monotonicity. Only partial answers are known to this question. For example, it is known that such a rule can be defined for approval-based party-list elections (see the work of Brill et al. [5]; mentioned in Sect. 4.4), but there is no clear generalisation of this rule to the setting of ABC rules. In case such a rule does not exist, it might be easier to first show that committee monotonicity and the core property are incompatible.

Q3 **The core property**: Does there exist an ABC rule that satisfies the core property (Definition 4.10)? Equivalently, is the core always non-empty? In case the core

© The Author(s) 2023
M. Lackner and P. Skowron, *Multi-Winner Voting with Approval Preferences*,
SpringerBriefs in Intelligent Systems, https://doi.org/10.1007/978-3-031-09016-5_7

can be empty, what is a sensible ABC rule that outputs a committee in the core whenever it exists? Can such a rule be computed in polynomial time?

Q4 **Analysis beyond the worst-case**: With a few notable exceptions, in Chaps. 3 and 4 we discussed axiomatic properties which are worst-case in spirit. A voting rule fails such an axiom even if there exist only few very unnatural election instances for which the property is not satisfied. An alternative approach would be to test if the properties hold for randomly generated instance of elections, or for elections from datasets containing real-life instance [14]. However, many common distributions of voters' preferences are too simplistic and do not capture the complexity of the voters' reasoning processes; the real election instances are rather scarce, and are collected in specific contexts, e.g., assuming that the voters' know the election rule that will be used to select winners. It is an important task to develop intermediate approaches that allow for a more fine-grained analysis and allow to understand which of the rules exhibit most desired properties on election instances that are likely to occur in practice.

Q5 **Relation between axiomatic properties and computability**: It is still unclear which combinations of axiomatic properties of ABC rules can be achieved in polynomial time. It is known that some rules are NP-hard to compute, but it is unclear which axiomatic properties of these rules cause computational hardness. For example, it is not known whether the axiom of FJR (see Definition 4.7) is satisfiable by a rule computable in polynomial time. Further, is there a polynomial-time computable ABC rule that is proportional (e.g., that satisfies PJR) and satisfies Pareto optimality? Or does there exist a polynomial-time rule that satisfies consistency and extends D'Hondt? (By Theorem 4.2, such a rule must violate either neutrality, anonymity, or continuity.)

Q6 **Preference data from distribution**: An important challenge is to prepare a representative database containing sample approval-based elections. Realistic probability distributions would allow for the automatic generation of synthetic (but meaningful) election instances, which are important for numerical simulations and performance tests of algorithms. In comparison to the ranking-based model, much fewer statistical models for generating approval-based elections are know. Further, it would be highly desirable to identify a set of distributions that are representative and that cover numerous potential types of voters and voting scenarios. A noteworthy attempt at creating such a representative collection of distributions has been made for the ranking-based model by Szufa et al. [19]. For ABC elections, this issue remains to be explored.

7.2 Further Open Problems

We continue with more specific or more technical open problems.

Q7 The key feature of Monroe's rule is its underlying assumption that a committee member can represent only 1/k-th fraction of the voter population. Monroe's rule could thus be generalised to many optimisation-based multi-winner rules by imposing the additional restriction that committee members can represent (i.e., derive score from) an α-fraction of voters. This idea resembles the group activity selection problem, where a set of activities is chosen, each of which has a maximum number of participants, and agents are assigned to activities subject to their preferences; see the survey of Darmann and Lang [10]. More generally, adding this "Monroe-style" constraint can be seen as requiring a homogeneous representation load among chosen committee members. This is a sensible assumption whenever candidates can satisfy only a limited number of voters (e.g., if candidates represent consumable goods). This idea of committees with homogeneous representation loads is largely unexplored.

Q8 Most axiomatic notions for proportionality are only applicable to ABC rules that extend apportionment methods satisfying lower quota (see Fig. 4.1). This excludes, e.g., ABC rules that extend the Sainte-Laguë method. As the Sainte-Laguë method is in certain aspects superior to the D'Hondt method (Balinski and Young [2] discuss this in detail), it would be desirable to have notions of proportionality that are agnostic to the underlying apportionment method.

Q9 What is the proportionality degree of rev-seq-PAV?

Q10 Does there exist an ABC rule that satisfies priceability and Pareto efficiency?

Q11 What is the computational complexity of verifying whether a given committee belongs to the core? Is it possible to find a committee in the core in polynomial time (if it exists)? In case of computational hardness, can the methods presented in Chap. 5 be used to obtain algorithms that are fast in practice?[1]

Q12 We have seen in Sect. 4.6 that proportionality and strategyproofness are typically incompatible. The corresponding impossibility result for arbitrary, i.e., irresolute, ABC rules [13] relies on Pareto efficiency. Since this is a property that many sensible ABC rules do not satisfy (see Sect. 3.2) it would be desirable to strengthen this result by relaxing this condition, e.g., by replacing Pareto efficiency with weak efficiency. Is this possible or are there ABC rules that are irresolute, strategyproof, proportional, but not Pareto efficient? Furthermore, both the result for irresolute [13] rules and for resolute rules [15, 16] rest on the assumption that the committee size k divides the number of voters. This assumption is unlikely to hold for large k and thus removing this assumption would be desirable.

Q13 A question related to monotonicity was asked by Sánchez-Fernández and Fisteus [17]: Is there an ABC rules that is proportional (even in a very weak sense,

---

[1] In a very recent preprint, Brill et al. [5] show that it is coNP-complete to verify whether a committee is in the core. Note that this does not rule out the the existence of a polynomial-time algorithm *finding* a committee in the core, as it is the case for EJR and PJR (cf. Sect. 5.3.1).

e.g., satisfying JR) and satisfies support monotonicity without additional voters (Definition 3.3)? As of now, AV and SAV are the only rules known to satisfy this property and both are not proportional.

Q14 Another question related to monotonicity concerns the Method of Equal Shares: while this method exhibits very strong proportionality guarantees (in particular EJR and priceability), it fails candidate monotonicity with additional voters (as discussed in Sect. 3.4). Is there an equally proportional ABC rule that also satisfies candidate monotonicity?

Q15 We mentioned in Sect. 3.1 that ABC rules that require tiebreaking do not satisfy neutrality (e.g., sequential and reverse sequential Thiele methods, Greedy Monroe, seq-Phragmén, and the Method of Equal Shares are not neutral). These rules can be made neutral with *parallel universes tiebreaking*: a committee is winning under the neutral variant if and only if it is winning for *some* tiebreaking order under the original rule. Parallel universes tiebreaking has been analysed for single-winner rules [4, 7, 11] but not for multi-winner rules. Such a modification will have an algorithmic impact (trying all permutations of candidates would require exponential time), but the exact computational complexity of these neutral rules is not settled. Further, under which conditions can these rules be computed in polynomial time?

Q16 In Sect. 5.1, we presented a coarse analysis of the computational complexity of ABC rules. This analysis could be refined by considering the CANDIDATE WINNER problem: given an election instance (A, k) and a candidate c, does there exist a winning committee W that contains c? This problem has recently be shown to be Θ_2^p-complete for Monroe and CC by Sonar et al. [18]. A similar analysis for other computationally hard voting rules (such as PAV) is missing.

Q17 Sequential PAV approximates the optimal PAV-score by a factor of at least $1 - \frac{1}{e}$. What is the factor for Reverse Sequential PAV? Is it better? The same question can be asked for other Thiele methods.

Q18 Several approximation algorithms and heuristics have been proposed for PAV, including seq-PAV, rev-seq-PAV, the approximation algorithm based on dependent rounding ([6], discussed in Sect. 5.2.3), and a local-search algorithm used for finding EJR committees in polynomial time [1]. The difference between these algorithms has not been investigated from a practical point of view. The main question is which of these algorithms should be chosen to approximate PAV given a very large election?

Q19 Is it possible to compute Thiele methods and Monroe's rule in polynomial time if the given preference profile belongs to the voter interval (VI) domain (see Sect. 5.2.4)?

Q20 The computation of some polynomial-time ABC rules can clearly be parallelised. For example, for AV each candidate can be processed independently of others. The framework of P-completeness [12] can be used to determine which ABC rules are inherently sequential (by showing P-completeness) and which can be parallelised (by showing, e.g., NL-containment). Such work has been done for single-winner rules [3, 8, 9] but not for multi-winner rules.

Q21 In real-life elections, it is sometimes required that each voter can approve at most k candidates. It is interesting to see what are the consequences of such a requirement in terms of qualities of the committees produced by various rules. Sometimes, it is even possible to distribute up to k points to candidates, i.e., to approve candidates more than once. This is clearly beyond the ABC model, but some concepts and results may transfer to such voting systems.

References

1. H. Aziz, E. Elkind, S. Huang, M. Lackner, L. Sánchez-Fernández, and P. Skowron. On the complexity of extended and proportional justified representation. In *Proceedings of the 32nd Conference on Artificial Intelligence (AAAI-2018)*, pages 902–909, 2018.
2. M. Balinski and H. P. Young. *Fair Representation: Meeting the Ideal of One Man, One Vote.* Yale University Press, 1982. (2nd Edition by Brookings Institution Press, 2001).
3. F. Brandt, F. Fischer, and P. Harrenstein. The computational complexity of choice sets. *Mathematical Logic Quarterly*, 55(4):444–459, 2009.
4. M. Brill and F. Fischer. The price of neutrality for the ranked pairs method. In *Proceedings of the 26th Conference on Artificial Intelligence (AAAI-2012)*, pages 1299–1305, 2012.
5. M. Brill, P. Gölz, D. Peters, U. Schmidt-Kraepelin, and K. Wilker. Approval-based apportionment. In *Proceedings of the 34th Conference on Artificial Intelligence (AAAI-2020)*, pages 1854–1861, 2020. Extended version at http://arxiv.org/abs/1911.08365.
6. J. Byrka, P. Skowron, and K. Sornat. Proportional approval voting, harmonic k-median, and negative association. In *45th International Colloquium on Automata, Languages, and Programming, ICALP 2018, July 9-13, 2018, Prague, Czech Republic*, volume 107 of *LIPIcs*, pages 26:1–26:14. Schloss Dagstuhl - Leibniz-Zentrum für Informatik, 2018.
7. V. Conitzer, M. Rognlie, and L. Xia. Preference functions that score rankings and maximum likelihood estimation. In *Proceedings of the 21st International Joint Conference on Artificial Intelligence (IJCAI-2009)*, pages 109–115, 2009.
8. T. Csar, M. Lackner, R. Pichler, and E. Sallinger. Winner determination in huge elections with mapreduce. In *Proceedings of the 31st Conference on Artificial Intelligence (AAAI-2017)*, pages 451–458, 2017.
9. T. Csar, M. Lackner, and R. Pichler. Computing the Schulze method for large-scale preference data sets. In *Proceedings of the 27th International Joint Conference on Artificial Intelligence (IJCAI 2018)*, pages 180–187. ijcai.org, 2018.
10. A. Darmann and J. Lang. Group activity selection problems. In U. Endriss, editor, *Trends in Computational Social Choice*, chapter 5, pages 87–103. AI Access, 2017.
11. R. Freeman, M. Brill, and V. Conitzer. General tiebreaking schemes for computational social choice. In *Proceedings of the 14th International Conference on Autonomous Agents and Multiagent Systems (AAMAS-2015)*, pages 1401–1409, 2015.
12. R. Greenlaw, H. J. Hoover, and W. L. Ruzzo. *Limits to parallel computation: P-completeness theory.* Oxford University Press, 1995.
13. B. Kluiving, A. Vries, P. Vrijbergen, A. Boixel, and U. Endriss. Analysing irresolute multiwinner voting rules with approval ballots via SAT solving. In *Proceedings of the 24th European Conference on Artificial Intelligence (ECAI-2020)*, volume 325 of *Frontiers in Artificial Intelligence and Applications*, pages 131–138. IOS Press, 2020.
14. N. Mattei and T. Walsh. Preflib: A library for preferences http: //www.preflib.org. In *Proceedings of the 3rd International Conference on Algorithmic Decision Theory (ADT-2013)*, pages 259–270, 2013.

15. D. Peters. Proportionality and strategyproofness in multiwinner elections. In *Proceedings of the 17th International Conference on Autonomous Agents and Multiagent Systems (AAMAS-2018)*, pages 1549–1557, 2018.
16. D. Peters. *Fair Division of the Commons*. PhD thesis, University of Oxford, 9 2019.
17. L. Sánchez-Fernández and J. A. Fisteus. Monotonicity axioms in approval-based multi-winner voting rules. In *Proceedings of the 18th International Conference on Autonomous Agents and Multiagent Systems (AAMAS-2019)*, pages 485–493, 2019.
18. C. Sonar, P. Dey, and N. Misra. On the complexity of winner verification and candidate winner for multiwinner voting rules. In *Proceedings of the 29th International Joint Conference on Artificial Intelligence (IJCAI-2020)*, pages 89–95. ijcai.org, 2020.
19. S. Szufa, P. Faliszewski, P. Skowron, A. Slinko, and N. Talmon. Drawing a map of elections in the space of statistical cultures. In *Proceedings of the 19th International Conference on Autonomous Agents and Multiagent Systems (AAMAS-2020)*, pages 1341–1349, 2020.
20. M. Brill, P. Gölz, D. Peters, U. Schmidt-Kraepelin, and K. Wilker. Approval-based apportionment. CoRR, abs/1911.08365v2, 2022. http://arxiv.org/abs/1911.08365v2.

Appendix A
Additional Proofs

In this appendix chapter, we provide some proofs and counterexamples that we were not able to find in the published literature.

In this appendix chapter, we provide some proofs and counterexamples that we were not able to find in the published literature. By default, we use alphabetic tiebreaking for ABC rules that require a tiebreaking order among candidates.

A.1 Additional Proofs from Chap. 3

Proposition A.1 *All Thiele methods with strictly increasing w-function as well as SAV satisfy strong Pareto efficiency; CC and MAV fail strong Pareto efficiency.*

Proof Observe that if W_1 dominates W_2 then the w-score of W_1 is strictly larger than that of W_2, due to our assumption that w is strictly increasing. Thus, W_2 is not a winning committee for these ABC rules. The same argument holds for SAV.

To see that CC fails strong Pareto efficiency, consider consider the approval profile

$$1 \times \{a, c, d\} \qquad 1 \times \{b, c, d\}.$$

For $k = 2$, $\{a, b\}$ is a winning committee even though it is dominated by $\{c, d\}$.

To see that MAV fails strong Pareto efficiency, consider consider the approval profile

$$1 \times \{a, c\} \qquad 1 \times \{b, c\} \qquad 1 \times \{d, e\}.$$

For $k = 1$, there is always one voter with Hamming distance 3 to any size-1 committee. Consequently, all size-1 committees are winning even though $\{c\}$ dominates $\{a\}$ and $\{b\}$. □

© The Author(s) 2023
M. Lackner and P. Skowron, *Multi-Winner Voting with Approval Preferences*,
SpringerBriefs in Intelligent Systems, https://doi.org/10.1007/978-3-031-09016-5

Proposition A.2 *CC, PAV, Monroe, Greedy Monroe, leximax-Phragmén, the Method of Equal Shares, and MAV do not satisfy committee monotonicity.*

Proof All counterexamples are implemented (and verified) in the abcvoting library [2].

First, let us consider the approval profile

$$2 \times \{a\} \qquad 3 \times \{a, c\} \qquad 3 \times \{b, c\} \qquad 2 \times \{b\},$$

CC, PAV, Monroe, leximax-Phragmén, and MAV choose $\{c\}$ for $k = 1$ and $\{a, b\}$ for $k = 2$.

For Greedy Monroe, consider the approval profile A defined as

$$A(1) = \cdots = A(6) = \{a\}, A(7) = \cdots = A(10) = \{a, c\}, A(11) = A(12)$$
$$= \{a, b, c\}, A(13) = A(14) = \{a\}, A(15) = \{a, d\}, A(16) = \cdots = A(18) = \{b, d\}.$$

We assume that Greedy Monroe breaks ties between candidates in alphabetic order and between voters in increasing order. For $k = 2$ groups have a size of 9, for $k = 3$ groups have a size of 6. Now, for $k = 2$, Greedy Monroe first chooses a and assigns voters 1–9 and then candidate b assigning voters $\{11, 12, 16, 17, 18\}$. For $k = 3$, Greedy Monroe first chooses a and assigns voters 1–6, then candidate c assigning voters 7–12, and finally candidate d assigning voters 15–18. We see that $\{a, b\}$ is not a subset of $\{a, c, d\}$.

For the Method of Equal Shares, consider

$$A(1) : \{a, d, e\} \qquad A(2) : \{a, c\} \qquad A(3) : \{b, e\} \qquad A(4) : \{c, d, f\}.$$

For $k = 3$, the budget of voters is 0.75. Candidate a is selected in the first round (due to alphabetic tiebreaking), reducing the budget of voters 1 and 2 to 0.25. Then candidate c is added (again by tie-breaking); the budget of voter 2 and 4 is decreased to 0. Only voters 1 and 3 have budget left. Candidate e is chosen last as the only remaining candidate with sufficient support. We see that the Method of Equal Shares selects the committee $\{a, c, e\}$.

For $k = 4$, the budget of voters is 1. In the first three rounds, candidates a, c, d, and e can all be chosen by two voters paying 0.5. By alphabetic tie-breaking, the Method of Equal Shares chooses a, c, d. In the fourth round, the remaining budgets are $0, 0, 1, 0$ for voters 1–4, respectively. Thus, in the last round, candidate b is chosen.

We see that the Method of Equal Shares selects $\{a, c, e\}$ and $\{a, b, c, d\}$ and is thus not committee monotone. Note that this example does not use the second phase of the Method of Equal Shares (based on seq-Phragmén) and thus works independently of the chosen method how to fill remaining committee seats (i.e., the second phase). $\qquad\square$

Proposition A.3 *Thiele methods, rev-seq-PAV, MAV, and SAV satisfy support monotonicity with additional voters; seq-PAV, seq-CC, seq-Phragmén, and leximax-Phragmén satisfy candidate monotonicity with additional voters but fail support monotonicity with additional voters. Further, Monroe, Greedy Monroe, and the Method of Equal Shares fail candidate monotonicity with additional voters.*

AV and SAV satisfy support monotonicity without additional voters; PAV, CC, seq-PAV, seq-CC, rev-seq-PAV, Monroe, greedy-Monroe, seq-Phragmén, leximax-Phragmén, the Method of Equal Shares, and MAV satisfy candidate monotonicity without additional voters; none of these satisfy support monotonicity without additional voters.

Proof All counterexamples are additionally implemented (and verified) in the abcvoting library [2].

Support monotonicity with additional voters: Sánchez-Fernández and Fisteus [6] show that Thiele methods, MAV, and SAV satisfy support monotonicity with additional voters (referred to as "support monotonicity with population increase" in their paper)

We prove that rev-seq-PAV satisfies support monotonicity with additional voters as well: Recall that rev-seq-PAV is resolute by definition. Let X be a subset of the winning committee and assume we add a voter approving X. We claim that exactly the same candidates are removed and in exactly the same order. Let us prove this by induction and assume it holds for rounds $m, \ldots, \ell$, where $\ell \leq m$ (recall that in rev-seq-PAV we count the rounds in the reverse order). As in rounds $m, \ldots, \ell$ the same candidates were removed, the marginal contribution of candidates outside of X is the same. The marginal contribution of candidates contained in X is larger. Consequently, the candidate with the least marginal contribution is the same as it was in the original election and thus not a candidate in X. We conclude that an additional voter approving X does not change the winning committee.

Janson [1] (based on Phragmén [5]) proves that seq-PAV, rev-seq-PAV, and seq-Phragmén satisfy candidate monotonicity with additional voters. Further, leximax-Phragmén satisfies candidate monotonicity with additional voters; this is a consequence of the fact that it satisfies weak support monotonicity with population increase [6], and the proof for seq-PAV in this paper also holds for seq-CC. A counterexample showing that seq-Phragmén fails support monotonicity with additional voters can be found in [1, 3]. Further, counterexamples for leximax-Phragmén and seq-PAV can be found in [6].

To see that seq-CC fails support monotonicity with additional voters, consider the following election instance:

$$3 \times \{a\} \qquad 1 \times \{a, c, d\} \qquad 1 \times \{b\} \qquad 2 \times \{b, c\}$$
$$1 \times \{b, d\} \qquad 2 \times \{c\} \qquad 2 \times \{d\}.$$

For $k = 3$, the winning committee according to seq-CC is $\{a, c, d\}$ (in order c, a, d, assuming alphabetic tiebreaking). If an additional voter approves $\{a, d\}$, seq-CC returns $\{a, b, c\}$ (in order a, b, c, assuming alphabetic tiebreaking) and hence seq-CC fails support monotonicity with additional voters.

To see that Greedy Monroe fails candidate monotonicity with additional voters, consider the following election instance:

$$
\begin{array}{cccc}
1 \times \{b, c, d\} & 1 \times \{a, c, f\} & 1 \times \{a, d, e\} & 1 \times \{c, e\} \\
1 \times \{a, b\} & 2 \times \{d, f\} & 1 \times \{b, e\} & 1 \times \{b, f\}.
\end{array}
$$

For $k = 3$, the winning committee according to Greedy Monroe is $\{b, e, f\}$. If an additional voter approves $\{e\}$, the winning committees changes to $\{b, c, d\}$. This committee does not contain e and hence Greedy Monroe fails candidate monotonicity with additional voters.

For the Method of Equal Shares, consider the following instance:

$$
\begin{array}{cccc}
1 \times \{b, d\} & 1 \times \{a, b\} & 1 \times \{b, d, e\} & 1 \times \{a, e\} \\
2 \times \{c, d, e\} & 1 \times \{c, e\} & 1 \times \{a, c, e\} & 1 \times \{b, c, d\}.
\end{array}
$$

For $k = 3$, the winning committee according to the Method of Equal Shares is $\{a, d, e\}$. If an additional voter approves $\{a\}$, the winning committee changes to $\{b, c, e\}$. As this committee does not contain a, the Method of Equal Shares fails candidate monotonicity with additional voters.

The Method of Equal Shares also fails candidate monotonicity with additional voters if only the first phase of the method is considered (i.e., the method may return fewer than k candidates). For the profile

$$
\begin{array}{ccccccc}
2 \times \{a, b, c\} & 1 \times \{a, g\} & 1 \times \{d, e\} & 1 \times \{b, d, f\} & 1 \times \{a, f\} & 1 \times \{h\} \\
1 \times \{a, h\} & 1 \times \{b, h\} & 1 \times \{b, d\} & 1 \times \{d, e, f\} & 1 \times \{c, e, h\}.
\end{array}
$$

The original winning committee is $\{a, b, e\}$. If an additional voter approves $\{e\}$, the winning committee changes to $\{a, d, h\}$ (assuming alphabetic tiebreaking). Thus, Equal Shares without the 2nd phase also fails candidate monotonicity with additional voters.

Finally, an example showing that Monroe violates candidate monotonicity with additional voters can be found in [6].

Support monotonicity without additional voters: AV and SAV satisfy support monotonicity without additional voters [6]. PAV, CC, seq-PAV, seq-CC,[1] rev-seq-PAV, Monroe, seq-Phragmén, leximax-Phragmén, and MAV satisfy candidate monotonicity without additional voters [1, 6].

To see that Greedy Monroe satisfies candidate monotonicity without additional voters, let c be a candidate in the winning committee. Now note that a voter additionally approving c can only lead to c being added in an earlier round. Hence, it is still contained in the winning committee (which may change, however). An analogous argument holds for the Method of Equal Shares as well.

---

[1] The proof is only stated for seq-PAV but holds for seq-CC as well.

PAV, CC, Monroe, leximax-Phragmén, and MAV do not satisfy the stronger axiom, i.e., support monotonicity without additional voters, as shown by Sánchez-Fernández and Fisteus [6]. Also seq-Phragmén fails this axiom [1, 3].

For seq-PAV, consider

$$
\begin{array}{llll}
1 \times \{c, d\} & 1 \times \{a, c\} & 1 \times \{a, d\} & 1 \times \{a, f\} \\
1 \times \{b, c\} & 2 \times \{b, f\} & 1 \times \{c, e\}.
\end{array}
$$

For $k = 3$, the winning committee according to seq-PAV is $\{a, c, f\}$. If the first voter changes her ballot from $\{c, d\}$ to $\{a, c, d, f\}$, the winning committee changes to $\{a, b, c\}$ (using alphabetic tiebreaking). Thus seq-PAV fails support monotonicity without additional voters.

For rev-seq-PAV, consider

$$
\begin{array}{lllll}
2 \times \{a, e\} & 2 \times \{b, c, d\} & 1 \times \{d, e\} & 3 \times \{c, e\} & 1 \times \{b, d, e\} \\
1 \times \{a, b, c\} & 1 \times \{c, d, e\} & 2 \times \{a, d, e\} & 1 \times \{b, d\} & 1 \times \{a, b\} \\
1 \times \{a, d\} & 1 \times \{a, b, d\} & 1 \times \{b, c\}.
\end{array}
$$

For $k = 3$, the winning committee according to rev-seq-PAV is $\{c, d, e\}$. If the first voter changes her ballot from $\{a, e\}$ to $\{a, c, d, e\}$, the winning committee changes to $\{b, d, e\}$. As this committee does not contain c, rev-seq-PAV fails support monotonicity without additional voters.

To see that seq-CC fails support monotonicity without additional voters, consider the profile

$$
\begin{array}{lllllll}
1 \times \{e\} & 1 \times \{a\} & 1 \times \{a, d\} & 3 \times \{b\} & 2 \times \{a, c\} & 1 \times \{b, c, d\} & 2 \times \{c\} \\
2 \times \{d\}.
\end{array}
$$

The winning committee according to seq-CC is $\{b, c, d\}$. If the first voter changes her ballot from $\{e\}$ to $\{b, d, e\}$, the winning committee changes to $\{a, b, c\}$. Candidate d is no longer contained in the winning committee, hence seq-CC fails support monotonicity without additional voters.

For the Method of Equal Shares, consider

$$
\begin{array}{llllll}
1 \times \{b\} & 1 \times \{a, b, e\} & 2 \times \{b, e\} & 1 \times \{c\} & 1 \times \{a, c\} & 1 \times \{a\}.
\end{array}
$$

The original winning committee is $\{a, b, e\}$. If the first voter changes her ballot from $\{b\}$ to $\{a, b, e\}$, the winning committee changes to $\{a, b, c\}$ (using alphabetic tiebreaking). This contradicts support monotonicity without additional voters.

For Greedy Monroe, consider $k = 2$ and

$$
A(1) : \{d\} \qquad A(2) : \{c\} \qquad A(3) : \{b\} \qquad A(4) : \{a, c\}.
$$

We assume alphabetic tiebreaking for candidates; for voters we assume that smaller numbers are selected first. The winning committee is $\{b, c\}$. If the first voter additionally approves $\{b, c\}$ (the new ballot is $\{b, c, d\}$, then b is selected in the first round (tiebreaking between b and c) and is assigned to voters 1 and 2. In the second round there is a tie between a, b, and c, and thus a is added to the committee. The winning committee is now $\{a, c\}$, which contradicts support monotonicity without additional voters.   □

Proposition A.4 *AV with a fixed tiebreaking order on candidates satisfies cardinality-strategyproofness and thus inclusion-strategyproofness. CC, PAV, seq-PAV, seq-CC, rev-seq-PAV, Monroe, Greedy Monroe, seq-Phragmén, leximax-Phragmén, the Method of Equal Shares, MAV, and SAV do not satisfy inclusion-strategyproofness.*

Proof To see that AV satisfies cardinality-strategyproofness, consider a fixed voter i. Observe that if i disapproves one of the (truly) approved candidates, say c, then it may cause at most one additional candidate getting into the winning committee. However, this will happen only if c is removed from the winning committee. In such a case, the satisfaction of i cannot increase. If i approves a not-yet approved candidate, then this might only cause that this candidate replaces some other candidate in the committee. Again, such a change cannot increase the satisfaction of the voter. Finally, a voter changing her ballot can be decomposed into a sequence of changes which consists of either approving a disliked candidate or disapproving a candidate that is actually liked. Each such a change cannot increase the satisfaction of the voter, as we have seen.

All counterexamples are also implemented (and verified) in the abcvoting library [2]. Note that inclusion-strategyproofness is defined for resolute rules; hence we assume lexicographic tie-breaking between committees for otherwise irresolute rules. For tiebreaking between candidates we assume alphabetic tiebreaking, as usual.

For CC consider the following profile with 5 voters:

$$1 \times \{a, b\} \qquad\qquad 3 \times \{a\} \qquad\qquad 1 \times \{c\}.$$

We assume an arbitrary tiebreaking between committees and without loss of generality we assume that a tie between committee $\{a, b\}$ and $\{a, c\}$ is resolved in favour of $\{a, b\}$. For $k = 2$, the winning committee according to CC is $\{a, c\}$ with a CC-score of 5. If the first voter changes her ballot from $\{a, b\}$ to $\{b\}$, committees $\{a, b\}$ and $\{a, c\}$ are tied with a CC-score of 4. By lexicographic tiebreaking, committee $\{a, b\}$ wins and the voter benefited from the manipulation.

For PAV consider the following profile with 6 voters:

$$1 \times \{c, d, e\} \quad 1 \times \{a, b\} \quad 1 \times \{b, f\} \quad 1 \times \{a, c, d\} \quad 1 \times \{b, c, f\} \quad 1 \times \{c, e, f\}.$$

For $k = 3$ the only winning committee is $\{b, c, f\}$. If the first voter submits $\{e\}$ instead of $\{c, d, e\}$, then $\{b, c, e\}$ will become the only winning committee.

For seq-PAV consider the following profile with 6 voters:

$$1 \times \{a, b\} \quad 1 \times \{b, d\} \quad 1 \times \{c, f\} \quad 1 \times \{a, b, f\} \quad 1 \times \{b, f\} \quad 1 \times \{b, c\}.$$

For $k = 3$ the winning committee is $\{b, c, f\}$. The first voter can successfully manipulate by changing her ballot to $\{a\}$—then the winning committee changes to $\{a, b, f\}$.

For seq-CC consider the following profile with 12 voters:

$$1 \times \{b, e, f\} \quad 1 \times \{a, b\} \quad 1 \times \{d, e, f\} \quad 1 \times \{d, e\} \quad 1 \times \{b, f\} \quad 2 \times \{c, d\}$$
$$1 \times \{a, b, c\} \quad 1 \times \{a, c\} \quad 1 \times \{a, b, e\} \quad 1 \times \{a, e, f\} \quad 1 \times \{b, c, d\}.$$

For $k = 3$ the winning committee is $\{a, b, d\}$. The first voter can successfully manipulate by changing her ballot to $\{c\}$—then the winning committee changes to $\{b, c, e\}$.

For rev-seq-PAV consider the following profile with 5 voters:

$$1 \times \{a, b, c\} \quad 1 \times \{b, d\} \quad 1 \times \{b, c\} \quad 1 \times \{a, d, e\} \quad 1 \times \{b, e\}.$$

For $k = 2$ the winning committee is $\{b, d\}$ (using alphabetic tiebreaking). If the first voter changes her ballot from $\{a, b, c\}$ to $\{a\}$, then $\{a, b\}$ will become the winning committee. The first voter prefers this committee to $\{b, d\}$, thus she has an incentive to misreport her preferences.

For Monroe consider the following profile with 12 voters:

$$1 \times \{b, d\} \quad 1 \times \{a, b, c\} \quad 1 \times \{b, e\} \quad 1 \times \{d, e\} \quad 1 \times \{e, f\} \quad 1 \times \{b, c, e\}$$
$$1 \times \{c, d, e\} \quad 1 \times \{b, c\} \quad 2 \times \{a, f\} \quad 1 \times \{b, c, d\} \quad 1 \times \{a, d\}.$$

For $k = 3$ the only winning committee is $\{a, b, e\}$. If the first voter changes her ballot to $\{f\}$, the winning committee changes to $\{b, d, f\}$.

For Greedy Monroe consider the following profile with 4 voters:

$$1 \times \{a, b\} \quad\quad 1 \times \{a, c, f\} \quad\quad 1 \times \{a, c, d\} \quad\quad 1 \times \{e, f\}.$$

For $k = 2$ the winning committee is $\{a, c\}$. If the first voter changes her ballot to $\{b\}$, then $\{a, b\}$ becomes the winning committee.

For seq-Phragmén consider the following profile with 6 voters:

$$1 \times \{a, b, c\} \quad 1 \times \{a, b\} \quad 1 \times \{b, f\} \quad 1 \times \{c, e\} \quad 1 \times \{b, e, f\} \quad 1 \times \{b, d, f\}.$$

For $k = 2$ the winning committee is $\{b, f\}$. If the first voter changes her ballot from $\{a, b, c\}$ to $\{c\}$, then the winning committee changes to $\{b, c\}$, an outcome that the voter strictly prefers to the original winning committee.

For leximax-Phragmén consider the following profile:

$$1 \times \{a, b\} \quad\quad\quad\quad\quad 3 \times \{b, c, d\}.$$

For $k = 3$, committee $\{b, c, d\}$ is winning with a load of 0.75 distributed to each voter. If the first voter changes her ballot from $\{a, b\}$ to $\{a\}$, then all committees are tied with a maximum load of 1. Due to lexicographic tiebreaking $\{a, b, c\}$ wins, which this voter strictly prefers to the original winning committee.

For the Method of Equal Shares consider the following profile with 6 voters:

$$1 \times \{b, c, d\} \qquad 1 \times \{a, b\} \qquad 1 \times \{b, d\} \qquad 1 \times \{c, d\} \qquad 2 \times \{d, e\}.$$

For $k = 3$ the winning committee is $\{b, d, e\}$. The first voter can successfully manipulate by changing her ballot to $\{c\}$—then the winning committee changes to $\{b, c, d\}$.

For MAV consider the following profile with 6 voters:

$$1 \times \{a, b, c\} \qquad 1 \times \{b, d\} \qquad 2 \times \{a, b, e\} \qquad 1 \times \{a, b, d\} \qquad 1 \times \{a, b\}.$$

For $k = 3$ the unique winning committee is $\{a, b, d\}$. If the first voter changes her ballot to $\{c\}$, then $\{a, b, c\}$ becomes the only winning committee.

For SAV consider the following profile with 2 voters:

$$1 \times \{a, b, c\} \qquad\qquad\qquad 1 \times \{d, e\}.$$

For $k = 1$ the winning committees according to SAV are $\{d\}$ and $\{e\}$; committee $\{d\}$ is chosen due to lexicographic tiebreaking. If the first voter changes her ballot to $\{a\}$, the winning committee will change to $\{a\}$, an outcome which is preferred by the first voter. $\square$

A.2 Additional Proofs from Chap. 4

Proposition A.5 *If k divides n, then Greedy Monroe extends the largest remainders method.*

Proof Consider an apportionment instance with p political parties, $C_1, \ldots, C_p$, and let n_i denote the number of votes cast on party C_i. Since n is divisible by k, Greedy Monroe always tries to assign a candidate to $\frac{n}{k}$ voters. Observe that:

$$n_i - \frac{n}{k} < \left\lfloor k \cdot \frac{n_i}{n} \right\rfloor \cdot \frac{n}{k} \le n_i.$$

Let $k_1 = \sum_{i=1}^{p} \lfloor k \cdot n_i/n \rfloor$. In the first k_1 rounds Greedy Monroe assigns to each party C_i exactly $\lfloor k \cdot n_i/n \rfloor$ seats. This is consistent with the first phase of the largest remainders method. During these rounds, whenever Greedy Monroe assigns a seat to a party, it removes n/k of its supporters. Then, each party C_i is left with less than $\frac{n}{k}$ supporters. Specifically, party C_i is left with the following number of supporters:

$$n_i - \left\lfloor k \cdot \frac{n_i}{n} \right\rfloor \cdot \frac{n}{k} = \frac{n}{k} \left(k \cdot \frac{n_i}{n} - \left\lfloor k \cdot \frac{n_i}{n} \right\rfloor \right).$$

Next, Greedy Monroe will assign the remaining seats to the parties in the order of decreasing values $k \cdot n_i/n - \lfloor k \cdot n_i/n \rfloor$, that is, it will proceed exactly as the largest remainders method. □

Proposition A.6 *In the general case (when k does not have to divide n), Greedy Monroe and Monroe do not extend the largest remainders method.*

Proof Consider an apportionment instance with 2 parties with, respectively, 50 votes and 31 votes. Assume the committee size is $k = 4$. For this instance LRM gives 2 seats to each party. Greedy Monroe can proceed as follows. It starts by giving the second party a representative and removing the group of 21 voters. Next it can give 3 representatives to the first party (depending on tiebreaking). The Monroe rule can also select 3 candidates from the first party and one candidate from the second party. □

Proposition A.7 *Greedy Monroe satisfies justified representation (JR).*

Proof Sánchez-Fernández et al. [7] show that Greedy Monroe satisfies PJR if k divides n, hence it also satisfies JR under this condition. However, Greedy Monroe satisfies JR also without this additional constraint. Assume towards a contradiction that Greedy Monroe fails JR for the election instance (A, k) and let W be the winning committee according to Greedy Monroe. As W does not satisfy JR, there exists a group of voters V of size at least n/k and a candidate $c \notin W$ approved by all of them. Adding candidate c would have increased the Monroe score of the committee by at least n/k in all rounds. Hence, the candidates contained in W also increased the score by at least n/k each. Thus, W has a Monroe score of n, i.e., all voters have an approved candidate in W, which implies that JR is satisfied. □

Proposition A.8 *An ABC rule with a proportionality degree of $f_R(\ell) = \ell - 1$ may fail EJR.*

Proof Consider the profile

$$2 \times \{a, b\} \qquad\qquad 1 \times \{c, d\}$$

for $k = 3$. An ABC rule that selects the committee $\{a, c, d\}$ fails EJR, but may have a proportionality degree of $f_R(\ell) = \ell - 1$. (To fully define such an ABC rule, it could behave as PAV on all other profiles.) □

Proposition A.9 *An ABC rule cannot satisfy both perfect representation and weak Pareto efficiency.*

Proof Consider the profile

$$2 \times \{a, c\} \qquad 1 \times \{a, c, d\} \qquad 1 \times \{a, d\} \qquad 1 \times \{b, d\} \qquad 3 \times \{b, c\}.$$

For $k = 2$, there is exactly one committee that satisfies perfect representation: $W_1 = \{a, b\}$. This committee, however, is dominated by $W_2 = \{c, d\}$. An ABC rule $\mathcal{R}$ satisfies PR if it exclusively returns committees satisfying PR; hence W_1 is the only winning committee and thus $\mathcal{R}$ fails weak Pareto efficiency. $\qquad\square$

Proposition A.10 *The proportionality degree of the Method of Equal Shares is between $\frac{\ell-1}{2}$ and $\frac{\ell+1}{2}$. The proportionality degree of SAV and MAV is 0.*

Proof For SAV fix $\ell \in \mathbb{N}$, set the committee size to $k = 2\ell + 1$, and consider the following profile with $m = 2k$ candidates and $n = k$ voters: the first ℓ voters approve candidates $a_1, \ldots, a_k$ and the next $k - \ell$ voters approve $b_1, \ldots, b_k$. SAV will select the committee $\{b_1, \ldots, b_k\}$. The group of the first ℓ voters is ℓ-cohesive, but no voter gets any representative in the elected committee.

For MAV fix $\ell \in \mathbb{N}$, set the committee size to $k = \ell + 1$, and consider the following profile with $m = 4k + 1$ candidates and $n = k$ voters: the first ℓ voters approve candidates $a_1, \ldots, a_k$ and the next voter approves $b_1, \ldots, b_{3k+1}$. MAV will select a k-element subset of $\{b_1, \ldots, b_{3k+1}\}$. The group of the first ℓ voters is ℓ-cohesive, but no voter gets any representative in the elected committee.

Finally, we consider the Method of Equal Shares. Since the method satisfies EJR [4] and EJR implies a proportionality degree of at least $f(\ell) = \frac{\ell-1}{2}$ [7], we get the lower-bound. For the upper bound consider the following instance. Fix $\ell \in \mathbb{N}$. We set $n = k = \frac{\ell(\ell+1)}{2}$ and $m = k + \ell$. The voters are divided into ℓ groups $N = N_1 \cup N_2 \cup \ldots \cup N_\ell$ such that $|N_i| = i$ for each $i \in [\ell]$. The set of the first k candidates is also divided into ℓ groups $C = C_1 \cup C_2 \cup \ldots \cup C_\ell$ such that $|C_i| = i$ for each $i \in [\ell]$. The set of remaining ℓ candidates is denoted by A. The voters from N_i approve C_i. Additionally the first voter from each group N_i approves A. The Method of Equal Shares can select the candidates from C_ℓ first. Then the voters from N_ℓ have no money left. Next the candidates from $C_{\ell-1}$ are selected, etc. Consequently, the method can return committee $C_1 \cup C_2 \cup \ldots \cup C_\ell$. Consider the voters who approve A. They form an ℓ-cohesive group, but the average number of representatives that they get equals $1 + 2 + \ldots + \ell = \frac{\ell(\ell+1)}{2}$. This completes the proof. $\qquad\square$

References

1. S. Janson. Phragmén's and Thiele's election methods. *CoRR*, abs/1611.08826, 2016. URL http://arxiv.org/abs/1611.08826.
2. M. Lackner, P. Regner, B. Krenn, and S. S. Forster. abcvoting: A Python library of approval-based committee voting rules, 2021. URL https://doi.org/10.5281/zenodo.3904466. Current version: https://github.com/martinlackner/abcvoting.
3. X. Mora and M. Oliver. Eleccions mitjançant el vot d'aprovació. El mètode de Phragmén i algunes variants. *Butlletí de la Societat Catalana de Matemàtiques*, 30(1):57–101, 2015.
4. D. Peters and P. Skowron. Proportionality and the limits of welfarism. In *Proceedings of the 2020 ACM Conference on Economics and Computation (ACM-EC-2020)*, pages 793–794, 2020. Extended version at https://arxiv.org/abs/1911.11747.
5. E. Phragmén. Sur la théorie des élections multiples. *Öfversigt af Kongliga Vetenskaps-Akademiens Förhandlingar*, 53:181–191, 1896.
6. L. Sánchez-Fernández and J. A. Fisteus. Monotonicity axioms in approval-based multi-winner voting rules. In *Proceedings of the 18th International Conference on Autonomous Agents and Multiagent Systems (AAMAS-2019)*, pages 485–493, 2019.
7. L. Sánchez-Fernández, E. Elkind, M. Lackner, N. Fernández, J. A. Fisteus, P. Basanta Val, and P. Skowron. Proportional justified representation. In *Proceedings of the 31st Conference on Artificial Intelligence (AAAI-2017)*, pages 670–676, 2017.

Printed in the United States
by Baker & Taylor Publisher Services